THE MORAY COAST, S
& THE CAIRNGORMS

JIMMIE MACGREGOR has been, amongst other things, a school-teacher, potter, author and illustrator, and was at the forefront of the British folk music revival in the 1960s. He became a household name through a long and successful partnership with Robin Hall, and a career which included radio and television programmes and performances all over the world.

Since 1982, he has presented his own daily radio show, *Macgregor's Gathering*, for BBC Scotland, and in the last few years has been realising an old ambition to make television programmes on the great outdoors. Jimmie is a keen naturalist and hill walker, and has broadcast radio series on the West Highland Way, the Speyside Way and the Southern Upland Way, in addition to a trip across Scotland with fellow naturalist Keith Graham. These programmes have been repeated several times, and in 1986 a very popular television series on the West Highland Way, presented by Jimmie, was shown on BBC Scotland. This was followed, in 1987, by an extended television version of the Speyside Way and Jimmie has plans for further televised walks.

THE MORAY COAST SPEYSIDE & THE CAIRNGORMS

JIMMIE MACGREGOR

BBC BOOKS

By the same author

Jimmie Macgregor's Folk-songs of Scotland (Volumes I and II)
Singing Our Own
Scottish and Border Ballads (with Michael Brander)
Macgregor's Gathering of Scottish Dialect Poetry
On the West Highland Way

Published by BBC Books
A division of BBC Enterprises Ltd
Woodlands, 80 Wood Lane, London W12 0TT
First published 1987
© Jimmie Macgregor 1987
ISBN 0 563 20560 1
Typeset in 11/12pt Bembo by Butler & Tanner Ltd
Printed and bound in England by Butler & Tanner Ltd
Frome and London

CONTENTS

v

ACKNOWLEDGEMENTS

M Y ENJOYMENT of the walk was increased enormously by the people I encountered along the Way, from fisherman Jim Slater at my starting point in Portsoy, to gamekeeper John McDonald, who stood with me on the summit of Ben Avon at the end of my jaunt. There were numerous friendly and interesting people in between, and I learned something from every one. My first walk along the Speyside Way was for a radio series which was produced by Chris Lowell of the BBC and researched by Kaye Coleman, and I am grateful also to Denis Dick, producer and station manager of the BBC in Aberdeen, for recognising the potential for a television series, and for allowing me to indulge myself on camera.

Filming requires a team, and mine, though small, was one of the best. Sandy Fraser, our electrician and general fixer, is a fine lad to have around – good humoured and with a strong back; and I had two ultra-professional cameramen in Ken Gow and Alistair Black. Alistair is built for the hills, with legs up to his oxters, and like Ken on the West Highland Way, was prepared to film from the most impossible angles and precarious positions. Debbie Black, our production assistant, would not describe herself as an athletic type, but kept up womanfully with everyone except our sound man, Jim Patchet. Jim is the only real mountain man among us, and his physique has the conformation of a whippet and the strength of a Shetland pony. All in all, a considerable team. I enjoyed working with them, and I'm glad to say that at the time of writing, another outdoor project is in the planning stages.

Picture Credits

All photographs taken by Jimmie Macgregor except:
BARNABY'S PICTURE LIBRARY pages 3 (Bill Meadows), 12 (Bill Meadows), 86 (P. Huggins) and 88 (R. Gee); JOHN CLEARE page 87; FRANK LANE pages 25 (Georg Nystrand) and 59 (B. S. Turner); C. P. LOWELL pages 13, 42 and 85; MORAY DISTRICT COUNCIL pages 23, 50 and 74; GEOFFREY N. WRIGHT page 15.

Front cover photograph by ALISTAIR SCOTT.

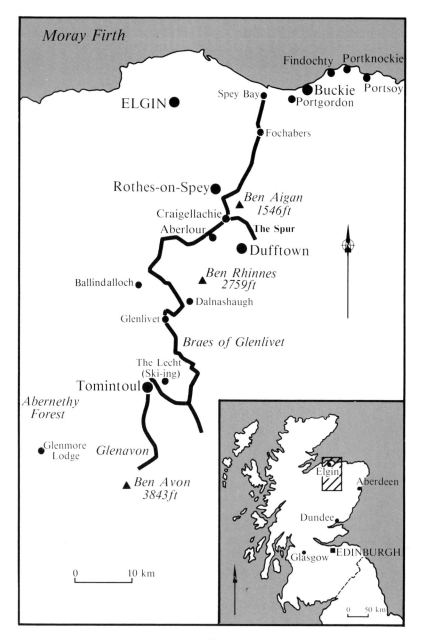

THE WALK

THIS BOOK is based on two journeys along the Countryside Commission for Scotland's Speyside Way. I walked the Way firstly for BBC Radio Scotland, and some time later, for my BBC Scotland 4-part television series, first televised in 1987. The planners of the original route ran into trouble with an obstructive landowner, and there is, in consequence, a gap between Ballindalloch and Nethybridge, with a proposed, but as yet undecided diversion over to Tomintoul. On both excursions I extended the walk by beginning on the Moray coast, to the east of the proper starting point at Spey Bay. My second outing took me by Tomintoul and the Lecht into Glen Avon, finishing at over 3000 feet on Ben Avon.

I have set out to describe for you the places I saw, the people I met, and the things I learned; so that the book is in no way intended as a guide, but rather as a collection of personal impressions and reflections.

A FEW DO'S AND DON'TS

DON'T TAKE on a walk like this unless you are reasonably fit. You don't have to be Ian Botham, or even Superman, but you really shouldn't be too out of condition. Your muscles will tone up after a few days, but you will certainly save yourself some discomfort by starting off in fairly good order. Do take care of your feet, and stop at the first sign of trouble. It may be courageous to slog on with painful blisters, but it's also daft, and can bring you to a complete halt. Much better to deal with problems immediately, and a basic foot kit is a useful addition to your equipment. This should include plaster in rolls (not the little stick-on bits), scissors, and chiropody felt to pad injured or sensitive areas. Footwear is of crucial importance, and much trouble can be avoided by the proper choice of boots. There are some marvellous designs now available which, though very light, are watertight, cool, and give support where it's needed. Take advice from your supplier, and buy the best you can afford. Try to avoid setting off in new boots, but if you must, they can be softened and made more flexible by the application of any one of a range of proprietary waxes and oils. Further comfort can be gained by using a shaped insole, and thin inner socks of cotton or fine wool under the heavier outdoor ones.

A bewildering variety of excellent rucksacks is now available, and again, take advice from your outdoor goods supplier. Don't waste money on one of those dinky little bags which hold a toothbrush, a chocolate bar, and one sock; but on the other hand, it's crazy to lumber yourself with a huge sack if you're only going to travel in short stages. Other useful items are whistle, torch, compass, camera and binoculars. It's pretty difficult to get lost on this particular route, but the Ordnance Survey maps of the area will provide a great deal of useful information. The Ordnance Survey maps you'll need are numbers 28, 29, 36 and 37 in the 1:50,000 series.

Accommodation is plentiful along the Way, and only at the Cairngorm end will the walker encounter any remote or exposed country. As more and more people take to outdoor pursuits, the care of the countryside becomes crucial. The idea should be to pass through with the minimum disturbance to plants, birds and animals, including farm stock. Gates should always be closed, except where the farmer has deliberately left them open, and fences, hedges, and farm equipment treated with respect. The countryside, which is our recreation, is other people's place of work.

PORTSOY: SAILORS, SERPENTINE, AND FISHER LASSIES

I T's difficult to believe that the picturesque but now rather quiet little village of Portsoy, with its jumble of attractive old buildings, was once a very significant port. For the best part of a hundred years, Portsoy enjoyed the benefits of a flourishing fishing industry, and after its decline a period of depression was relieved in some measure by the village's understandable popularity as a holiday resort. Beeching's butchery of the railways in the 1960s set that back, until growing car ownership brought the return of the visitors in good numbers.

Portsoy

The harbour built by the Earl of Seafield in the 1820s proved to be a failure, and was replaced by the present one, which coped with the massive traffic of the flourishing nineteenth-century fishing industry. Still a good harbour, it is now relatively little used.

Many people are familiar with Portsoy marble (serpentine) in the form of tourist trinkets, but the quarrying and working of the marble were once so important that the Scottish parliament banned the importation of foreign marble. This arrangement lasted until the union with England in 1707, when the law was changed, to the considerable detriment of Portsoy and Scotland. However, if the English were not impressed, the French were: Portsoy marble is to be found in the Palace of Versailles, built by Louis XIV.

On my first visit to Portsoy, I made my way up from the shore to meet a man who was a part of the village's more recent history.

Jim Slater, like many of the old-timers of the fishing communities, is a good story-teller, with an easy and colourful style of speech, enhanced by a rich north-eastern accent. He has that combination of ruggedness and gentleness which seems to be characteristic of people who face the elements every day. He worked at herring and line

3

fishing from 1920 right through to the beginning of the Second World War. Nowadays, he told me, although the men still live in the villages along the coast, the boats of the north-east are mainly at Fraserburgh, Aberdeen and Peterhead, and the new fishermen buzz along to these places in their dormobiles and mini-buses. Today's successful fisherman lives in a comfortable modern home, and is quite at ease with the Mercedes, and the wildly expensive fishing vessels and equipment. Jim Slater's best year was 1924, when he earned £53 for sixteen weeks' work. He was delighted to get so much, and his catch was talked about for some time: 'Most of us were content to make enough to support our families and pay our bills.'

Jim accepts that the life was hard, but like every fisherman I've ever met, he loved it, and wouldn't have had it any other way; for though there was drudgery and bone-aching toil, there was a measure of freedom, good companionship, and constant change.

In the summer the boats went to Shetland, Orkney and the northern waters; then in the autumn down to Lowestoft and Yarmouth. The fisher lassies followed the fleets to do the gutting and packing: 'We couldn't have done without them, and there's no doubt that they sustained the industry.' Jim told me that when the women went on strike in Lerwick in the early Twenties, everything came to a standstill. The mystery is that strikes were not commonplace, for the women and girls were always underpaid, and sometimes worked in truly awful conditions. At the time of the Lerwick strike, a three-woman team of two gutters and a packer was paid one shilling (five new pence) for a barrel of herring. A barrel held three hundredweight.

In Shetland, the women lived in tiny huts in teams of three, although it was common for teams to double up, with six workers crammed together in appalling accommodation. Each fisher lassie had her kist (chest) of belongings which travelled with her, and the kist would often provide the only furniture on a dirt floor, serving as both table and chair.

Summer conditions were tolerable, but Jim Slater remembers the lassies working in Lowestoft and Yarmouth in all weathers, often starting before daybreak and finishing after dark. The only source of heat and light was the bubbly lamp, a sort of watering-can arrangement filled with fish oil, and with a long wick in the spout. The guttering flame created more evil-smelling smoke than light, but despite all this, plus the routine cuts from razor-sharp gutting knives in salty, half-frozen hands, the Scottish fisher lassies were famous for their good humour, entertaining themselves with their favourite Sankey revival hymns, old Scottish airs, and fishing songs.

The Herrins' Heids

Fit'll we dee* wi' the herrins' heids?
Fit'll we dee wi' the herrins' heids?
We'll mak them for loaves and sell them for breid.
Herrins' heids and loaves o' breid,
And a' sorts o' things.

> CHORUS:
> O' a' the fish that swim in the sea,
> The herrin' it is the fish for me.
> Sing fal lal lalido, fal lal lalido,
> Fal lal lalido, iday.

Fit'll we dee wi' the herrins' eyes?
Fit'll we dee wi' the herrins' eyes?
We'll mak them for puddings and sell them for pies.
Herrins' eyes, puddings and pies,
Herrins' heids, loaves o' breid,
And a' sorts o' things.

> CHORUS.

Fit'll we dee wi' the herrins' fins?
Fit'll we dee wi' the herrins' fins?
We'll mak them for needles and sell them for pins.
Herrins' fins, needles and pins,
Herrins' eyes, puddings and pies,
Herrins' heids, loaves o' breid,
And a' sorts o' things.

> CHORUS.

---

* *Fit'll we dee* = What'll we do

Another song which is very popular in the north-east is *Tatties**
and Herring. I learned it some years ago from a gentle giant called
Charlie Simpson. Charlie was a policeman, and when he wasn't
throwing trees and large chunks of metal around at the highland
games, he played guitar and sang Scottish folk songs. He knew that
there was a verse about the Russians, but couldn't remember the
words, so I made my own.

Tatties and Herring

The auld fisher folk they dinna think shame,
On a Setturday nicht when they drink a' the ale;
Then Sunday comes roon' and there's no' muckle* carin',
For the rest o' the week they'll get tatties* and herring.

> CHORUS:
> Tatties and herring, tatties and herring,
> The lads are weel fed apon tatties and herring.

When the king wanted men tae conquer his foe,
It was neither tae Lowestoft or Yarmouth he'd go;
He cam' tae the north for the willing and daring,
The lads that are fed apon tatties and herring.

> CHORUS.

The bold Russian army, they said tae their czar,
'The lads frae the north-east we'll no' face in war;
Ye can cry us a' fearties*, but man, we're no' carin',
For yon lads are fed apon tatties and herring.'

> CHORUS.

Wi' a poond in the week may ye aye be content,
Ten shillings tae lay by for claes* and the rent;
Hauf a croon tae lay by, for when ye're no' farin',
And seeven and sixpence for tatties and herring.

> CHORUS.

---

* *tatties* = potatoes *muckle* = great, big *fearties* = cowards *claes* = clothes

CULLEN: KINGS AND COOKING

FROM PORTSOY almost all the way to Spey Bay and the official starting point of the Speyside Way, the walk follows a cliff-top path, and the walker is always within exhilarating sight, sound and smell of the sea. From Portsoy to Cullen is only a few miles, and one passes between the bay of Sandend and the village of Sandend itself. Only visitors call Sandend Sandend. The local folk call it something that sounds like – well, I don't quite know what it sounds like, but it doesn't sound like Sandend. I was to discover that all along the coast: place names were rarely pronounced as they looked on paper.

On none of my Scottish walks have I approached a tourist office for information. They undoubtedly do a fine job, but I prefer to talk to people who live in the area, and in Cullen I was lucky enough to be able to pick the brains of two very knowledgeable men, railway buff Douglas Berry, and the Reverend John Guthrie, a keen local historian. The first thing I learned from John was that the spectacular rock formations on the sands of Cullen Bay take their name from the legendary three kings of Cologne, being known locally as the three kings of Cullen. John also explained the layout of the little town, which slopes steeply to the sea, and is neatly divided into the upper town and the lower seatown by the imposing railway viaduct. The lower town is an appealing sprawl of small houses, beautifully painted, some with gable ends to the sea for protection against the weather, the rest pointing in any and every direction. In the upper town, all is order, space and light, and this is no accident.

The old village of Cullen was a little way inland, and adjacent to Cullen House. The Earl of Seafield was not too happy about the proximity of the peasantry, and between 1822 and 1830 Cullen was rebuilt on its present site. Very pleasant it is too, with a good square, and the broad main street running down to the sea, while orderly rows of secondary streets go off at right angles. The place is also immaculately clean, in common with all the villages along the Moray coast.

Whilst in Cullen, I took the opportunity to call on Peter Perrit, an old art school colleague, who, with his wife Yvonne, runs the cosy little Bayview Hotel. In an upstairs corridor, I was surprised to recognise a portrait of Dorothy, wife of the Scottish painter James Morrison. The painting, which is a prized possession of Peter's, goes back to student days, and Peter was pleased that I had identified it. Before leaving the Bayview, Peter and Yvonne insisted that I try a bowl of the local delicacy, Cullen Skink. Skink is a kind of fish soup and, properly prepared, is quite delicious. Here is a basic recipe:

Cullen Skink

1 large finnan haddie (smoked haddock)
1 medium-sized onion, chopped
3 cups milk
1 oz butter
8 oz mashed potato
Salt and pepper
Anything else you fancy, if it's fishy

Put the haddock in a shallow pan, and add enough water to cover it. Bring to the boil and simmer for about 15–20 minutes, by which time it should be easy to remove the skin and bones. Put the fish, with the water in which it was cooked (now a good fish stock), the chopped onion, and the fishy anything-else-you-fancy into a saucepan, put on the lid, and simmer for another 20 minutes or so, until the onion has softened. Add the mashed potato, butter and the milk gradually, stirring well, until the soup is as thick as you like. Season the whole thing with salt and pepper.

This is just what the doctor ordered for a tired walker at the end of a long day – a cross between a soup and a stew. Delicious.

After calling on another old friend, John Duguid, late of the wonderfully musical Royal Jubilee Arms Hotel at Cortachy, near Kirriemuir, and now presiding over the rather grand Seafield Arms, I climbed up the embankment to the viadict to meet Douglas Berry. The view is impressive, and Douglas informed me that we were about 150 feet up. The line that came across here was part of the Great North of Scotland Railway from Aberdeen to Inverness. Douglas rather worried me by remarking that the huge arch on which we stood replaced one which had fallen; and although he assured me that the present structure was filled solidly with concrete, I took this information as my cue to move on. The viaduct is now stabilised and maintained by the local council. The old permanent way makes a splendid, well-drained path, and I was soon on my way to Portknockie, at the western end of Cullen Bay.

PORTKNOCKIE:
A SEA DOG AND A FUNNY FIDDLE

PORTKNOCKIE IS built around a natural harbour, and unlike most of the other fishing villages, the houses do not come down to the sea, but are strung along the cliff top. It's a perjink* wee place, and has a freshly painted and newly scrubbed look. Cornwall is the only other place in Britain where I have seen such colourful houses. Everything is painted – doors, window frames,

Portknockie harbour

---

* *perjink* = neat, trim

9

A painted house, Portknockie

lintels, stonework, pointing, pipes and gutters – and one house can have as many as five or six colours. The result should be a visual disaster, but strangely, the overall effect is quite delightful.

After chatting to a couple of fishermen who had just landed a good catch of crabs, I was taken by a group of local schoolboys to see Bow Fiddle Rock, a great stone archway rising from the sea, and loud with the cries of fulmar, kittiwake and herring gull. The lads were on holiday, and it seemed to me that they were what boys should be. They were obviously good pals, they had a collie with pale blue eyes – a strange kind of sea dog – and their playgrounds were the cliffs, the harbour, and the fishing boats. Not a bad way for a boy to live.

Portknockie has seen its fine harbour bristling with the masts of the old sailing ships, followed by the steam drifters; and now the pleasure craft, with only the odd fishing vessel. On leaving the Portknockie boys, I had a wander around the trim, well-laid-out streets, before taking once again to the cliff path which would take me on to Findochty and Buckie.

The Portknockie boys

FINDOCHTY: SPOONER, HAP, SCRAMBLE, CACK AND SAMMO

INDOCHTY DOESN'T sound like Findochty. It's pronounced Finechty, or Finichty; and according to Spooner Smith, one of the most colourful characters in a colourful place, even the -y at the end of the name is different from all the -ie endings on the coast because the BBC came along many years ago and poshified it. Findochty is possibly the most attractive of all the villages, and is now being carefully protected. As Tam Robertson told me, brandishing a revolting bucket of bait under my nose the while: 'It's a grand wee place. We've no' even a pub here, and I think we'll jist keep it that way.' Tam's real name is William Smith Robertson, but, 'Naebody in the place wad ken* me by that.'

---

* *wad ken* = would know

Findochty

Until the decline in fishing on the Moray coast, Findochty nurtured generations of fishing folk. There are records of the fishing industry back into the sixteenth century, and with such a natural harbour, there is little doubt that men went to sea from here long before then. The village is immortalised by James Clarke Hook's painting, *Home with the Tide,* dated 1880, which hangs in the Tate Gallery.

Wandering around the village, my eye was caught by the complete wheelhouse of a fishing boat which had been manhandled into a garden, where it somehow looked quite natural, and perfectly suitable as a potting shed-cum-conservatory. At the far end of the harbour, I had an interesting and entertaining conversation with some of the local veterans – tough philosophical men who had spent their lives at sea, and were now in their seventies and eighties. Spooner Smith, the most talkative of the group, reminisced about changes in the village, and in seafaring. He also tried to explain for me the strange nicknames, or 'T' names, of the area. His mates were Gordon Murray, Magnus Work from Orkney, Harold Durno (not a fisherman, but a cooper), Jim Robertson and Alec Bruce; the T names included Hap, Scramble, Cack and Sammo, and, of course, Spooner himself. Spooner is named after an old-time footballer, and he told me that when his mother was carrying him, someone 'clapped her oan the belly' and said, 'I'll bet you have a right wee Spooner there.' Spooner is rather proud of the fact that he had his T name before he was born. People can go through life among the fisher folk known only by their T names, the origins of which are often quite forgotten. It was explained to me that 'Hap' was so called because he always gave a lusty rendering of 'O Happy Day' on his way up to the church on the headland. Religion was, and still is, important to the fishing communities, and one of the features of Findochty is a sculpture of a fisherman, with the inscription, 'They see the works of the Lord, and his wonders on the deep.'

The author with Spooner

BUCKIE: BOATS, BUILDERS, AND THE TWA HORNS O' THE DE'IL

UCKIE, I was pleased and mildly surprised to learn, sounds exactly like Buckie. It is approached from the east by way of Portessie, which does not sound remotely like Portessie, being known locally as the Sloch. A sloch, I discovered later, is a bay or inlet.

The most striking things about Buckie (apart from the fact that it is the biggest and busiest place I had so far seen on my route) are the two main churches. The steeple in Cluny Square marks the North Church, while its Roman Catholic equivalent features famous twin spires, known to some of the sterner adherents of other persuasions as 'The twa horns o' the De'il*'. The Reformation was strongly resisted in this area, and Catholicism survived under great pressure. The persecution of Catholics was severe, and the first Catholic church to be built after the Reformation was burned down by a rampaging mob. A barn which was later used as a place of worship was also destroyed. Since 1755, Catholics have used, at first secretly, a simple stone cottage. It stands inland not far from Buckie, and although it is known to some as the Banffshire Bethlehem, it is very easy to miss, the only distinguishing mark being a stone globe on one of the gable ends.

Buckie's harbour is a colourful confusion of boats and tackle, and on the quayside there is much shouting and to-ing and fro-ing. The confusion is illusory, for this is a busy work place, with a lot of skilled people in action. I watched in lip-chewing suspense as a skipper turned a 70-foot-plus vessel on its axis in the crammed harbour, with a few inches to spare at bow and stern; and all casually done while he chatted and joked with one of the crew. Shellfish are now the mainstay of the industry in Buckie, and the catches are processed in the town, mainly for export. The fishing grounds of the Buckie fleet are 80 to 120 miles out to sea.

There was a time when no ship would sail from any of the harbours along this coast on a Sunday, but things are different now. In the splendidly appointed wheelhouse of his co-owned boat *Rival,*

---

* *twa horns o' the De'il* = two horns of the Devil

Buckie harbour

Alistair Reid, a courteous, quietly-spoken man, explained that the investment required of the modern fisherman is so great that boats and crew must work to maximum capacity. Most of the craft in Buckie's harbour are valued at between £500,000 and £1,000,000, which explains why they are normally owned by partnerships or families.

Buckie also builds boats, and Bill Cowie, who seems to know just about everything that goes on in the town, showed me a beautiful 75-footer which was nearing completion. The builder was Willie Thomson, an old school friend of Bill's, and the vessel was for a Buckie buyer. Willie Thomson had also made a superb replica of Henry Bell's *Comet*, which was built in 1812 to serve the Clyde coast and Mr Bell's hotel at Helensburgh. The copy was ordered by the shipbuilding firm of Woods in Port Glasgow, and it is still on prominent display in the town, close to the main through road.

Sandy Sutherland is a well-known and much respected spokesman for, and representative of, the fishing industry, and I met him on both my visits to Buckie. There is little that Sandy doesn't know about the politics and economics of fishing, but, remembering my conversation with the old boys at Findochty, I wanted to know if Sandy thought that today's fisherman had it easier than his predecessors. He pointed out that as the inshore fishing grounds have mostly been cleaned out, the lads have to go further out, and spend longer days at sea. The rewards for the successful could be great, but the outlay and risks were massive. The most important investment that the fisherman makes in the industry is himself, and no matter how great the skill, and refined the equipment, luck and the elements still play their part.

I asked Sandy about the fisherman's traditional observance of superstition. He replied that, like most modern sea-going men, he didn't believe in such rubbish, but didn't take any chances; and if he heard anyone whistling on board, he would remind them that the last thing required at sea was extra wind.

Some time ago, a poem on the subject of luck was sent to my BBC radio programme, *Macgregor's Gathering*. It was written by Peter Buchan, a well-known poet of the north-east. It's called *Kirkyaird Rain*.

Kirkyaird Rain

I'm thinking back on Davy.
He'd aye his ain luck.
Wi' canny speed he'd forge aheid
When ither folk were stuck.
'Though better men than Davy
Could get nae fish ava*;
The cod wad steer for Davy's gear,
And gie themselves awa*.

---

*ava = at all   awa = away

But let's be fair tae Davy.
It wisna Davy's blame
That tempest wild lay meek and mild
'Til Davy had won hame.
And though ye'll 'gree that Davy
Had better luck than maist;
Ye'd surely say, this very day,
'We kent* it couldna laist.'

We're here tae bury Davy,
There's mair than hauf the fleet.
A teemin' sky – still, Davy's dry,
And we're a' dreepin' weet.

PORTGORDON: RAILWAYS, MORE RAILWAYS, AND FREE WHISKY

BUCKIE IS the last place of any size before Spey Bay, and after passing through Buckpool, which had an earlier harbour than the one at Buckie, I found myself on the road to Portgordon.

Portgordon is another of those little places which was once quite important. It was founded in 1797, had a good fleet, and carried on a healthy trade with the Baltic, exporting grain and fish, and bringing in salt and coal. This is a pleasant enough part of the walk, running parallel with and very close to the sea, but where possible I avoid walking on made-up roads, so I was glad to meet Douglas Berry once again and to leave the tarmac. Douglas was to tell me more about the region's railway system, so we crossed the road, went under an arched bridge, and climbed the steep embankment which took us up on to the old track.

My first visit to this place was in high summer, and I remember that the wild area behind the bridge was a riot of colour, with thistle, dandelion and rosebay willowherb in bloom, as well as mallow,

*kent = knew

17

ragged robin, ragwort, knapweed and vetch among many others. The charm of the place was enhanced by the sounds of linnet, yellowhammer, chaffinch, goldfinch and wren. Douglas was less interested in all this than in telling me about his beloved railways, and he explained that at one time Banffshire, Moray and Nairn were very well served. The Great North of Scotland Railway, which had a branch on Speyside, faced severe competition from the Highland Railway, and even the little village of Portessie had two stations. In 1860 the Inverness and Aberdeen Junction Line extended its influence by opening the Inverness and Perth Junction Railway; so that in the peak period, the whole of the north-east was criss-crossed by lines serving the needs of fishing, agriculture and the whisky industry.

The Scottish tourist boom in the Victorian era, inspired to a great extent by Queen Victoria herself, and by the romantic novels of Walter Scott, added greatly to the prosperity of the lines. Local landowners were quick to see the commercial possibilities, and were involved from the beginning. On Speyside, some of the distilleries had their own lines and shunting yards. Whisky travelling on open wagons in great wooden casks was at some risk; for if a train had to make a stop, it was not uncommon for the local lads to get underneath with a brace and bit.

The decline in the railways of the north-east was a long and gradual one, but it had already begun in the years following the First World War. The reasons were various, among them the slump in fishing, increased motor car ownership, and improved roads; and, of course, Lord Beeching, who closed lines, and left communities all over Britain virtually stranded. The last train to serve the distilleries made its final journey in 1968, but at Boat of Garten near Aviemore, enthusiasts can now enjoy the spectacle of beautifully restored engines and rolling stock on the move once more.

TURNED STONES, WADERS AND FLYERS

L EAVING PORTGORDON, I looked forward to a quiet and leisurely plod along the shore line to Spey Bay. I am a compulsive beachcomber – if anything so pleasantly time wasting can be called compulsive, and I can happily spend several hours pottering on a few hundred yards of shingle, so I did not establish any speed records on this stretch. There were many diversions. A school of dolphins disported themselves close inshore, and a pair of black-backed gulls pirated sand eels from the terns which had done all the hard work in catching them. This is also a great place for waders, especially late in the season, when birds like the curlew and redshank, which have nested inland, come to exploit the rich resources of the tides. I spent some time watching a group of feeding turnstones trotting down the sand on blurred, clockwork legs, one inch behind the receding waves, and running back up one inch ahead. Turnstones come to these shores late in the season from their nesting grounds in places like Greenland and Iceland. We usually see them in slightly tatty condition from the autumn moult, but in breeding plumage the turnstone is a handsome bird, in black, white and chestnut. Its bill is shorter and sturdier than that of most waders, and the bird does indeed turn stones in its search for food.

I was totally absorbed in the wildlife activity around me, and in the fascinating debris of the foreshore, and I was really startled by a huge shadow swooping over the stones. What was this? An albatross? An eagle? Superman? No – a glider. I watched through my binoculars for some time, and marvelled at the near vertical climb, then the silent, circling search for the thermals which lift the craft higher and higher. I decided to investigate further and, by following my nose, found myself at Dallachy, and the site of the Highland Gliding Club.

I made myself known to the club's treasurer, Anne Burgess, and in turn was introduced to a charming woman called Angie Veitch, who works as a biochemist in Inverness. Anne is the chief tourist officer for Moray District Council, and both women are dedicated to gliding. As chief flying instructor at Dallachy, Angie explained for me the basic principles of the sport, and then suggested, as I feared she would, that I should try it for myself. Great was my relief when it became clear that we would be in a two-seater, with Angie very much in control. Such was her air of confidence, and so obvious her expertise, that I felt completely relaxed as we began our run on the end of the towing cable.

Angie had told me that a glider gains height faster than a jet plane,

Angie Veitch with the author at Dallachy

and I believed her as I suddenly found myself looking straight up at the sky. There was a thoughtful moment when the tow line fell away, and we momentarily stood still in mid air. Just as I was becoming resigned to the fact that we must fall back tail first, the nose dipped and we were gliding. Unhooked, I was instantly hooked.

There was a wonderful feeling of buoyancy and lift, and the only sound was the strangely soothing 'whoosh' of the glider through the air. Angie explained that in still air, the craft loses height at a predictable rate, and the idea is to use the available time to move from thermal to thermal. The thermal is a column of warmer air which pushes the glider ever higher, and the skilled pilot reads the landscape and the sky for signs of these thermals. Some of the updraughts are very narrow, and at times, we tipped over at what seemed to me to be an impossible angle, so that we were almost revolving on one wing tip as we spiralled upwards. The experienced glider pilot uses the air currents in exactly the same way as the birds, and Angie remembers sharing a very small thermal with an osprey which had been fishing in Spey Bay. She described it as a wonderful experience, as the great bird wheeled around only a few feet away, obviously perplexed by this vastly greater bird invading its air space.

There was more sensation of real flying in that short flight than I've had in hundreds of thousands of miles by jet.

SPEY BAY:
A NICE COURSE AND AN ICE HOUSE

T HE DISTANCE from the Highland Gliding Club at Dallachy to Spey Bay is not great, but my progress was slow. I still couldn't resist the temptation to stop and examine every piece of sea-borne debris, from the mundane to the exotic. Sad, dismembered limbs of plastic dolls, and a huge balk of timber from a pier. Glass bottles worn to grey-green opacity by months or years of sand and sea. Dead birds of all kinds. A crate of boxed dates, well salted. Great limbs of trees polished and bleached to the colour and texture of bone, and bone buffed to the sheen of porcelain.

Spey Bay is a modest cluster of buildings, the most imposing of them being the Spey Bay Hotel. This replaces one which burned down in 1965, and is owned by a large, genial and hospitable man called George Christie. George is a well-known local businessman, one of whose interests is the Spey Bay golf course, which he leases from the Crown. The Crown Estates acquired the land in 1936 from the Duke of Gordon, who surrendered it in payment of death duties. As George walked me round the course, I realised that although it is certainly not the grandest in this country of fine golf courses, it must surely be one of the most attractive. On one hand is the sea with a grand open view north over the Firth to the blue-grey distances of Sutherland and Caithness; on the other, the River Spey; and all around are whins* and woodland. Skylarks sing overhead, and the nineteenth hole awaits.

Golf has been around here for a very long time, with courses at Buckie, Elgin, Keith and Cullen; and the Cullen Kirk session records report that as long ago as 1641, some baddies called Duffus and Stevenson broke the Sabbath for a game of golf.

At the turn of the century, the present course was known as the links. It was used for grazing, and was no more than a jumble of sand dunes covered in rough grasses and whins. All this changed on 10 September 1907, when the course was officially opened by the Duke of Richmond and Gordon, to the enthusiastic cheers of a huge crowd.

---

* *whins* = gorse

The course was designed in one afternoon by Mr Ben Sayers, who took a couple of hours to walk around inspecting the ground, and another couple to mark it out with flags, completely ignoring problems like the massive whin bushes. Someone else could deal with that. The course was originally named Tugnet Golf Club, but as Spey Bay Golf Club, it is today much as Ben Sayers envisaged it. The beauty of the setting, and the increasing ease of travel by rail and car, ensured the club's success. The Duke established a family holiday cottage here, and in the 1920s Ramsay MacDonald was a regular visiting player, and presented the club with a handsome trophy.

Moving up to the river mouth, I kept a sharp look-out for an old friend called Tom Howe, whom I had met on my first walk in this area. As I crossed the wooden footbridge by the first Countryside Commission for Scotland's Speyside Way markers, Tom was approaching on the river path. I noticed that he had made an addition to the family since our last meeting. This was Kirsty, a seventeen-week-old, hyperactive little West Highland terrier, who whirled around Tom's heels like a windblown snowflake. Tom Howe was in charge of the fishing here for many years, and still loves the place, though he regrets the passing of a whole way of life. At one time there were fourteen fishing crews here, plus fly nets and a sea drag. There is now only one coble netting crew on the river, and its future looks uncertain. The coble is a flat-bottomed boat used for taking salmon and sea trout. The technique is simple but effective. The team tows the boat upriver, walking in single file on the shingle. The boat makes a sweep with the net, which is then hauled in by hand. All hard physical work. At the end of the netting season, this part of the river is then fished by the Speymouth Angling Association.

No one seems to understand exactly why the salmon stocks are decreasing, but Tom Howe feels that drift netting and even long line fishing at sea are taking too many fish before they can get to the rivers to breed. The young salmon moves out to sea where it stays for several years before maturing and returning to the river of its birth. A great deal of attention is being paid to the problem of decreasing stocks, and at the Knockando hatcheries, six million salmon eggs are hatched each year. Spey Bay has been associated with salmon fishing as far back as the fourteenth century.

Tugnet ice house

An interesting relic is the old Tugnet ice house, over the door of which is a stone bearing the date 1830. It's an odd-looking building with a triple-arched roof. It is now used as a fishing museum, but at one time it was packed with ice, and thickly covered with turf to keep the salmon fresh in summer. Before the development of ice houses, salmon was preserved by part cooking and pickling.

The ice house at Tugnet is unusual in that it is preserved in good condition, but ice houses were widespread in the eighteenth and nineteenth centuries, and in common use until the First World War. The Tugnet example was probably always one of the best. Quite often, they would consist simply of a deep cellar or part of a cellar, suitably adapted. Disused wells were also used, and these could have been the models for the vertical ice houses, which were bottle shaped and sometimes between 20 and 30 feet deep. The most common type was a simple square underground building with a vaulted roof thickly covered in living turf. These later became more sophisticated, some even having a double skin for insulation.

The big cities were already importing ice for use in the confectionery trade, but in rural areas, the ice house was usually built on raised ground near a pond, although shallow ice pans were often specially dug. In winter, the ice was broken up with hammers, and carried to the ice house by horse and cart. The landed gentry, eager to indulge a new-found continental taste for ice cream, chilled fruit and other delicacies, sometimes had two or three ice houses tastefully incorporated in their landscaping. There are probably many undiscovered and unsuspected ice houses in Scotland, hidden under grassy, shrub- or tree-covered mounds.

THE RIVER, AND THE RETURN OF THE FISH HAWK

THE SPEY is a big powerful river carrying a mass of detritus, and the brown staining of the water can be seen several miles out into the Moray Firth. Where the fresh water meets the salt, there is an abundant supply of food, and birds gather in great numbers and variety. The force of the tide and of the river itself means that the banks of shingle at the river mouth are continually changing their conformation, and it has been necessary on several occasions to break through the build-up of shingle to allow the river free passage to the sea.

The area around the mouth of the river supports a wonderful variety of wildlife, and Tom Howe enthused about being able to sit at his own window and observe the fox, badger, mink and otter, the roe deer raiding his neighbour Sandy Paterson's neeps, and the osprey coming down for his breakfast. The vast range of species owes its existence to the diverse habitat. There is the agricultural land with its fields and hedgerows, the wetlands, and the areas of scrubby growth, as well as the big trees of the more mature woodland. The river is deep and fast-flowing in some places, shallow and still in others, with islands of constantly changing size and shape. In a very short time I was able to identify an exciting variety of birds, and a botanist would be drooling at the profusion of growth. One strange little plant is scurvy grass, so-called because the sailors used to eat its leaves and flowers to prevent scurvy on long voyages. All the common birds are to be seen, and in the first mile or so along the river bank I saw two sparrowhawks: a female flying into a deep wood, and, a little later, the much smaller male zipping along a

Young osprey

hedgerow, obviously intent on mugging some unsuspecting dun-
nock or yellowhammer.

The most striking and spectacular bird to be seen here is the
osprey, and it's worth making the journey to Speyside for that alone.
Ospreys spy out and pursue from a considerable height the fish
which are their diet, and the plunge and the kill can be breathtaking.
The only bird in the sky of similar size, if we ignore the great gulls,
is the buzzard, but the osprey's flight is more dashing, and its
silhouette contrasts rakishly with the buzzard's broad-winged stock-
iness. The osprey is the only true fish-eating bird of prey we have
in this country, and the story of its persecution and reappearance in
Scotland is full of contradiction – demonstrating as it does stupidity,
insensitivity and callousness, as well as compassion, appreciation of
beauty, and skill and determination.

The osprey suffered in Scotland from the old notion that anything
with a hooked beak should be classified as vermin and wiped out –
an idea that still hasn't quite died. The bird lays a particularly beautiful

egg, and as persistent persecution reduced it to a comparative rarity towards the end of the last century, fanatic collectors went to incredible lengths to steal the eggs, reducing the population still further. Ospreys return to the same location year after year, and the best known of the old nest sites was on the tower of the ruined castle on an island in Loch an Eilein in the Forest of Rothiemurchus. The birds are known to have nested there at least as far back as the turn of the nineteenth century. They never seem to have been plentiful, though there were nests at Loch Insh, Loch Morlich and in the Abernethy Forest. In the years before their eventual disappearance, the ospreys were continually harried, birds being shot and eggs taken; and in 1899 the last attempt at nesting was made at Loch an Eilein. It was unsuccessful, and the osprey ceased to be a breeding bird in Scotland, though migrant wanderers were occasionally seen.

Fifty years were to pass before the great fish hawk was to re-establish itself. It was in the early 1950s that observers felt that the birds might be marking territories once again on Speyside. Several nesting attempts failed, and in 1958, despite a round-the-clock vigil by volunteers, a vandal climbed the tree, broke two eggs which contained partly formed chicks, and left some painted hens' eggs in their place. However, in 1959 the ospreys bred successfully in a pine tree at Loch Garten, and with the occasional minor setback, have done so ever since.

The Royal Society for the Protection of Birds quickly abandoned the idea of attempting to keep the site secret, and boldly decided on maximum publicity instead, a policy which has been outstandingly successful. They arranged, with the enthusiastic co-operation of the Seafield estate, to set aside almost 700 acres around the nest site as a wildlife sanctuary. For protection, the lower branches of the nest tree were removed; the base was protected with barbed wire; and a twenty-four-hour watch was set up during the breeding season. A public information centre and observation post was then established, with powerful binoculars through which hundreds of thousands of people have been able to watch the intimate lives of these wonderful birds.

The success story continues. There is now another visitor centre near the nest at the Loch of the Lowes, and ospreys breed at several places in Scotland. I know two sites where nesting ospreys can be seen from the car, on main roads. However, there is no room for complacency. The osprey is a migratory bird, travelling to North Africa each year, and there are losses, especially among young birds. Shooting, a few seasons of bad weather, or nests being blown down could seriously damage what is still a relatively small population. The great fish hawk is still in need of our protection, and one way in which you could help would be by joining the Royal Society for the Protection of Birds.

SWALLOWTAILS AND A GOOD PLAN

WALKING ALONG the River Spey is quite delightful, with something to engage the attention every step of the way. The going is easy on the old fishermen's paths and good progress is possible, but I don't believe in hurrying in a place like this, preferring to keep my eyes and ears open and binoculars at the ready. An extremely impressive landmark here is the Spey viaduct. It is just under 1000 feet in length, and sturdy enough to withstand the river's occasional ferocious spates. The viaduct was constructed in 1886 and carried the Great North of Scotland Railway. It now provides a convenient footpath to the village of Garmouth on the other side of the river.

I was enjoying the peace and tranquillity of the riverside path, accentuated rather than disturbed by the sound of water and bird song; but as I moved along I gradually became aware of a screeching cacophony, rapidly increasing in volume as I drew near. The source of the frantic racket was a colony of terns on a shingly island – close to the bank, but separated from it by a deep channel of powerfully rushing water. Protection enough. A fellow concealed in the undergrowth of the bank, and studying the birds intently through powerful glasses, turned out to be one Alastair Smith, a retired police inspector. This was a fortuitous meeting for me, as Alastair is an acknowledged expert on terns and was able to tell me quite a lot about this particular colony.

Crammed together on these few yards of shingle, in uneasy company with about twenty pairs of common gulls, were a hundred pairs of terns. The terns were of two species in equal numbers: the common tern and the Arctic tern. Most people have seen these lovely little birds fishing, usually fairly close to shore. They are even smaller than the little black-headed gull, and much more delicate in build and outline. Their wings are long and curved, and they have the distinguishing feature of a fine, trailing forked tail, which explains why they are sometimes called sea swallows.

The two species are similar, but as Alastair pointed out, there are distinguishing features. In the common tern, the bill is orange, and in its Arctic relative, it is blood red. The Arctic also has a longer and more delicate trailing forked tail. Beautiful in the air, it looks a bit daft on the ground, for its poor wee legs are ridiculously short, giving it a comically stumpy look.

The terns winter in Africa, and arrive at the mouth of the Spey around the middle of May. Over a period of years, this colony has gradually moved from Spey Bay to its present location about two miles upriver. Shore-nesting terns are often washed out by the tides, and even here on the river, nests are sometimes destroyed by spates. The birds seem strangely insensitive to the hazards of their chosen sites, and Alastair Smith has noticed that the oystercatcher, which nests in the same kinds of places, always seems to lay just above the high-water mark. Alastair's theory is that the oystercatchers, which do not migrate, get to know the river better than the terns.

The colony presents a wonderful spectacle, and the birds are close enough to be seen in some detail. Through binoculars one can examine individual feathers, and spot the beady eye of a chick peering out from under the wing of a brooding mother. The birds start laying very soon after their arrival, and incubate for about twenty-two days. The second broods start to appear several weeks later and by this time the colony has everything from eggs to downy chicks, to huge fat fledglings bigger than their parents but as yet unable to fly. Each pair of terns claims a territory extending to only a few inches around the nest, but that tiny space is desperately defended, with much squawking and flapping.

Alastair drew my attention to two large birds standing away at the extreme end of the stony spit – great black-backed gulls, as big as an osprey, and much more dangerous to the tern colony. They will wait patiently for hours, then make a rush and a pounce, and a gull or tern chick will disappear down that huge gaping bill. Alastair says that they will even tackle the biggest fledglings, holding them fast by a wing and battering them to death. Having seen them deal with an adult puffin on St Kilda, I wasn't surprised. Some naturalists say that these huge piratical gulls are the most destructive predators we have among the birds.

By the end of July, the hectic business of the breeding season is over for the terns, and they will move out into the Moray Firth to feed, remaining there until the end of September or early October, steadily building up strength and reserves of body fat. Suddenly, they're gone, and on their way to the warmer waters and easy pickings of Africa, leaving behind on the silent shingle the odd egg shell, and a few fluttering feathers.

The river bank seemed strangely quiet as I left the terns behind and made my way along the fishermen's paths towards Fochabers. Not far from the terns' island, I came upon a spot called Cumberland's Ford. This is where the Duke of Cumberland – Sweet William to the English, and Stinking Billy to the Highlanders – crossed the Spey on his way to the fateful field of Culloden. The ford was also used some time earlier by the Jacobite troops led by Prince Charles Edward Stuart.

Just outside Fochabers, I was directed by a signpost to leave the riverside path and take to the road. I wasn't too keen on this, but the local laird, who owns most things around here, has decreed that Speyside Way walkers are not allowed to use this section of the river path. Perhaps the Duke simply wants to ensure that we have a good view of the entrance to Gordon Castle, for the road takes the walker past the war memorial and the great drive leading to the enormously imposing gates which open into the castle grounds.

In the late 1700s, the village of Fochabers was immediately adjacent to the castle. This didn't appeal to the fourth Duke of Gordon, so he had the whole place razed, and rebuilt on its present site. The result is splendid. The village has an air of space, leafy serenity, wide streets, low buildings, and sparkling cleanliness. The layout was planned by a man called John Baxter, and he provided a fine square, a gridiron street plan, and fine solidly built domestic and civic buildings. Many of these two-hundred-year-old structures are now protected by conservation orders, and there is a fine folk museum.

Entrance to Gordon Castle, Fochabers

The high school in Fochabers owes its existence and its name to the fact that a man called Milne refused to have his hair cut. He was dismissed from the laird's employ for this offence, left Fochabers, and went to New Orleans. He was responsible for building most of the harbour there, made a fortune, and bequeathed £15,000 to build the school which now bears his name.

The building I favoured was the Gordon Arms, where I refreshed myself, and ran into an old friend called Alex Jenkins. Alex is much involved in the traditional music of the area, and is a champion player of the moothie (harmonica to you). He is a weel kent face around the folk festivals in places like Keith, Auchtermuchty and Kinross. His moothie, or moothamonium as it is known in some high-toned circles, is an impressive instrument, which looks rather like a giant corn cob. It consists of six harmonicas radiating from a central core, and a spin of the wrist gives Alex instant access to six keys. One of the girls in the hotel found me a battered old guitar, and Alex and I entertained the bar for a while. Of the tunes we played, the only ones I remember are *The Barren Rocks of Aden,* and *Jock Cameron,* but there were many more.

Fochabers is a particularly fine example of a planned village, but it is by no means unusual. By the end of the eighteenth century there were more than two hundred similar villages in various parts of Scotland. The layout was based on an even earlier model, for Scotland's medieval towns had a main central market street, with cowgates running off at right angles. The cowgates were just that: streets used to get the cows into the marketplace. When Grantown-on-Spey was rebuilt about 1765, the people carried their Mercat Cross from the old village, and re-erected it in the new.

Fochabers, Keith and Aberchirder in Banffshire, and Stuartfield and New Deer in Aberdeenshire, among many others, were (usually) built at the bidding of the local lairds. The gentry wanted an impressive approach to their grand houses, and the original clusters of grubby hovels were a distinct embarrassment, so the lairds advertised plots of land, and even offered prizes of money and medals to anyone who could produce an acre of good corn. There were awards, too, for good-quality textiles, for beekeeping, and good building; but whatever the motivation for the planned villages, they were very successful, and today are a pleasure to look at and to live in.

BRAMBLE JELLY AND ROCK PUDDING

THE BREAKFAST waiter in New York's Waldorf Astoria was probably rather bemused by the delighted reaction of the two Scottish guests when offered a selection of the hotel's preserves. There was, to be sure, a fine choice: blackcurrant and strawberry jams, Scotch orange marmalade, Deeside heather honey, and wild bramble jelly. What the waiter didn't know was that the preserves were manufactured by Baxters of Fochabers in Scotland, and that the couple were Gordon and Ena Baxter. Gordon Baxter's Speyside produce is now known world-wide, but he has never become blasé or uncaring. That may be because Baxters of Fochabers has existed for more than a hundred years, and is still a family business.

It all started in George Baxter's village grocery in Spey Street, Fochabers, and it was the enterprise of Mrs Margaret Baxter which

Baxter's village shop

was to lead to the flourishing modern complex which now stands just outside the village on the banks of the Spey, and sends its high-quality foods to more than sixty countries. In the little spare time she had, Margaret Baxter began to produce jam from locally collected fruits. It was made in the back shop, and sold over the counter in front, in solid two-pound stoneware jars. From the beginning, the Baxters used only the best raw materials and gave good value. It worked. Success was immediate, though modest, and the Baxters began to develop a range of quality foods. Their son William and his wife Ethel maintained and improved those standards, and Baxters is now a model complex of well-designed buildings housing the factory, restaurant, shop and craft centre, in skilfully landscaped grounds.

Gordon and Ena, and Gordon's brother Ian and his wife Margaret are proud of their humble beginnings, and give pride of place to the splendid replica of the original shop in Spey Street. It's an attractive and interesting building which incorporates the old containers, fittings and implements of George and Margaret Baxter's day. Gordon Baxter is a very busy man, and I asked him why, in view of his success, he didn't lie back a bit, enjoy his fishing and take it easy. He has rejected no less than 123 take-over bids, some of them very generous indeed, but he explained that, like the rest of the family, he is committed to maintaining standards, and to the welfare of the 500 people employed by Baxters. Gordon and Ena refer to them, not as employees, but as helpers. They feel that to sell out to a faceless multi-national company with no feeling for the place, the people, or the traditional values of Baxters, would be unthinkable. I hope that they will continue to believe that.

With a promise from Gordon to take me on the river and show me what Spey casting is all about, I left Baxters, to the music of the resident piper, Jimmy Purdie. Like most people at Baxters, Jimmy does more than one job, for when he's not piping, he's in charge of boiling the beetroot. I'm no judge of a boiled beetroot, but I was assured that he does that just as well as he plays the pipes. Finally, allow me to offer a word of advice. Never begin a meal with Baxters Royal Game Soup. Everything that follows will be an anti-climax.

The Way rises quite steeply out of Fochabers towards Ordiequish, but the uphill slog is rewarded by splendid views opening up across the Spey valley, and from this elevation, one can really appreciate

Ordiequish

33

the lushness of the river land. After a couple of miles, a Forestry Commission sign catches the eye, and the walker is led into a little glade high above the water. There is a notice which warns, 'Have care, steep slopes,' and they really are precipitous, though the path, perhaps 200 feet or so above the Spey, is quite safe. This is a beautiful spot and ideal for a breather. There are some really grand old conifers,

Earth pillar at Aultderg

well mixed with other tree species and shrubs. It was a breathless, baking, bee-humming day on my first visit here, and the air was tangy with the resinous smell of the pines, combined with countless perfumes from flowers, shrubs and broad-leaved trees.

It's well worth following the path downwards for a few hundred yards to where there is a view of the famous earth pillars of Aultderg. These geological curiosities are huge pillars of a kind of sandstone conglomerate – a sort of mixed rock pudding. They are thousands of years old, and were formed by a capping stone protecting them from the erosion going on around them, gradually creating the great reddish columns which now stand clear of the steep banks. The capping stones are long gone, and it's possible to observe the effects of erosion on the crowns of the pinnacles.

On leaving Aultderg, the road continues to rise quite steeply through very pretty country, still with the wide views of the Spey valley on the right. I was rather surprised to find the Way going straight through some farm buildings, and it occurred to me that I shouldn't much fancy people traipsing through my back yard. William Burgess, who farms at Woodhead, doesn't seem to mind. He told me that after the 'lang haul' up from Fochabers, a few of the walkers call in for a drink, so I suppose it's just as well that, as yet, the way is not very much used. William Burgess is an open, friendly character, strong and squarely built. He is the type once described by an Aberdonian friend of mine as being 'beef doon tae the heels'. In an area, and an era of specialised farming, William chooses to diversify. His farm is fairly high and he has a lot of steep ground, so large machinery is not very suitable, but as William observed, cattle can take grass off a hill much more effectively than a machine.

As the farm is just about on the edge of the whisky country, and quite remote, I asked William about illicit distilling. He believed that some of the older folk in the hills might remember such things, but didn't think there had been any activity for a long time. 'About three weeks, you mean?' I suggested. Slight pause, then, 'Not guilty!'

ON THE RIVER WITH HAIRY MARY AND THE MEDICAL PRACTITIONER

THE PROMISED day on the river with Gordon Baxter was a revelation. My life has always seemed too busy for leisurely pursuits like fishing, but I now fully understand the attraction, and for the first time I comprehend what lifelong fishermen mean when they say that catching a fish is only a small part of the total experience. Everything about the pursuit of fishing is pleasing. We fished a spot where fast white water ran into lovely broad slow moving pools. On one hand the bank was sloping and grassy, and on the other, great rocks overhung the water, partly obscured by trees and shrubs which were full of small birds. The fisherman is surrounded by elements which are soothing to the eye and ear. Bird calls and the continuous background music of the water, the lowing of distant cattle, and the friendly presence of an old dog combine to create a calming reflective atmosphere. The most important factor, I believe, is the total absorption which fishing seems to demand and create. This next pool will be the one. Perhaps this fly rather than that. And the conviction that the next cast will be utter perfection. If not that one, then the one after that.

As we arrived at the river, the rain had just begun, but it soon settled to a dour drizzle which was unrelenting all day. I didn't mind a bit, and in no time at all, I was totally absorbed. Gordon had found me some waders, and with my old tweed hat and oiled jacket, I was well protected and looked the part. That was all, I'm afraid, for even with the expert instruction of Gordon, and ghillie Keith McLaren, I discovered that the Spey cast is as difficult as it looks easy. Keith and Gordon raised the rod in a leisurely easy way, and the line described a graceful S, just touching the water before snaking out to drop the fly well upstream. The idea then is to let out the line and allow the fly to drift down with the current, over the spot where you judge your fish to lie.

On my first ever Spey cast, executed with more sinew than style, the hook and fly whizzed round and whopped me on the back of the head. My technique deteriorated from then on, but, soaking wet, surrounded by midges and nearly waist deep in water, I'd happily have stayed there until dark. Indeed, on the same stretch of the river there was an elderly chap who had come from South Africa to fish the Spey. He was on the river all day, the rain didn't let up, he never caught a fish, and he was rapturously happy.

Keith McLaren, the ghillie on this stretch of the river, is an expert. He knows every pool, every current, and where the fish will be lying at a given time, or in specific climatic conditions. His job is to ensure that his clients catch fish. He advises them on where to go, and when. He instructs in technique, where necessary, and suggests the appropriate fly. The man who can design a good and effective new salmon or trout fly is assured of immortality, at least among fishermen; and the art of tying a fly is much admired and envied. There is a story of an old ghillie who was asked by the laird to tie a selection of flies for the coming season. After a few nights, the laird came round and expressed disappointment at how few had been completed. 'Och, I'm doing my best, Your Grace,' said the old fly man. 'But they're so realistic that as soon as I have them finished, the spider is stealing them from under my nose.'

Fishing flies are beautiful things, and their names I found very intriguing. There's the green highlander, the blue charm, the Jeannie, thunder and lightning, and Hairy Mary. Some are named after people, like the Jock Scott, or the Willie Gunn, a well-known fisherman from the Helmsdale area. There's the stoat's tail, the silver stoat, the fiery stoat and the black doctor. A lot of well-known fishermen were, and are, doctors, and, it seems, not above using a prawn or shrimp type of lure which is illegal in fresh water. That one is known as the medical practitioner.

As I left the water and stumbled up the bank in my oversized waders, I could distinctly hear the sound of salmon sniggering behind my back, but I didn't care. I had a few questions to put to Gordon Baxter. The Spey is a world-famous salmon river, but I had been hearing mutterings about it not being quite as good as it used to be. Gordon, however, seemed cautiously sanguine. 'This year is better than last, and last year wasn't too bad.'

One thing Gordon did notice was a seasonal change. In his youth, the Spey was an early river, most fish being caught in April, May and June. Now, the best times are from mid July until the end of the season. There is, however, general concern about the diminishing number of fish. Gordon pointed to several reasons, the most important being that far too many are lost at sea, on the way back from their feeding grounds off Greenland and north of the Faroes. Salmon must return to the river of their origin to breed, and if they are prevented from doing so in sufficient numbers, the decline in population is dramatic. Other problems are fixed nets along the coastline, and over-fishing in the estuaries, preventing many fish getting up-river. I suggested that the man who was netting for a living surely deserved at least as much consideration as the sportsman. Gordon readily agreed, but pointed out that rod fishing brings about £150 million per year to Scotland. A good answer, if the question is purely economic.

I left the river, and the men of the river, with one question quite unanswered. Why is it that the salmon, which never feeds while in fresh water, can be taken on an artificial lure?

UP AND DOWN TO CRAIGELLACHIE: BIRDS AND BRIDGES

FROM WILLIAM BURGESS'S farm to the next stop on the Speyside Way, Boat o' Brig, is a fairly short step; hilly, but lovely walking. Boat o' Brig is so called because when the old bridge collapsed, a ferry took over until the replacement was built. There are now two bridges here, for road and rail cross the Spey at this point, the road being the B9103 from Rothes to Keith. There is a very small lay-by for two or three cars, and from this point, steps lead up through some trees and on to the open hill.

At the foot of a steep but well-made path, I found a notice which reads, 'Please keep to the path. All dogs to be kept on lead. If gate is closed, wait here. Stock being herded.' I know that there are some outdoor people who look on signs like these as some kind of dreadful visual pollution, and a threat to freedom, but I can't agree. There is a vast difference between an open hill or moorland, and areas which are being farmed. It's obvious that dogs can disturb stock, but people sometimes forget that damage can be done in other ways too – things like wire fences cost a great deal of money, and should be treated with care. If you have to go through a gate, make absolutely certain that it's closed behind you; and if you're forced to go over it, don't

Boat o' Brig

put your weight on the latch end. Keep close to the hinges – it puts less strain on them. I won't even mention litter. If you're the kind of person who reads this book, I'll take it for granted that you don't throw rubbish around the countryside.

A friend of mine who is fanatical and obsessive about litter is Molly Porter, who was the countryside ranger on the Speyside Way. Molly goes around picking up minute scraps of debris which are almost invisible to the naked eye, and although I did make fun of her mania, I really wish there were more people like her. Molly accompanied me on this stretch when I made my first walk. She is an experienced ranger with all the outdoor skills, including mountain rescue, but she was new to the Speyside Way when I first met her, on a previous walk, and it was interesting to hear her opinion of the route.

Molly was very much struck by the variety and contrast along the Way, and by the richness of the plant, animal and bird life. She told me she had encountered problems with the signposting, although she is obviously well used to finding her way around. The timber of the Countryside Commission for Scotland's Speyside Way markers is stained a dark brown and treated with creosote. The actual directions are also very discreet. The idea is that they should harmonise with their surroundings; but Molly felt that they succeeded rather too well, as she at first found herself sailing past them and covering quite a bit of extra distance. Molly advises walkers to equip themselves with the Ordnance Survey map, and with the very attractive and informative leaflets issued by Moray District Council. The leaflets give a description of the route with some background information, and advise on accommodation. Camping is unrestricted on the route, camp sites are being designated for groups, and Molly told me that the waiting room and ticket office of the old railway station at Blacksboat is being converted to provide bunkhouse facilities.

Molly Porter is a lean, leggy person, and set a cracking pace up through the forest to the highest point on this section. We arrived at the crest of the hill in superb conditions. The visibility was perfect and we could see the Spey winding ahead towards Ballindalloch, while, looking back along the route, Tugnet and Spey Bay were clearly visible, and out across the Moray Firth, the dim blue hills of Sutherland. All around was the wide spread of the Spey valley, and it was easy, as we looked at the rich land, to see why this area is known as the breadbasket of Morayshire.

We coasted downhill towards Craigellachie, through wonderful mature woodland which contained many fine broad-leaved trees as well as the coniferous species. Moray is one of the most densely forested areas in Britain, and timber has always been important here. After the great fire of London in 1666, the Rothiemurchus estate provided timber for London's new drainage system. The huge trees were logged, and bored out with hot irons, before being floated down the river and shipped out from Garmouth. During the London blitz, some of these old timbers were exposed, and found to be still in good condition, and bearing the Rothiemurchus estate's mark.

The old forest is still in good heart, and offers a wonderful habitat for a great variety of insect, bird and animal life. All the common Scottish woodland creatures are here, fox, badger, stoat, weasel, roe deer – and one can also see the increasingly rare red squirrel in one of its remaining strongholds. The woods are full of tits, robins, warblers, and all the small birds that one would expect in such a place; but there are also siskins, and the exotic crossbill. This last is a really splendid bird, the male in rosy red plumage, and the female in green. The crossed mandibles of the rather parrot-like bill are specially adapted for extracting the seeds from pine cones.

Stars of the show, however, are two very contrasting birds. The first is the tiny crested tit, which is quite unknown in many parts of Britain, and the second is the 'horse of the woods', the capercaillie. The capercaillie is a really huge bird, the male being fully the size of a hefty turkey, and nasty with it on occasions. In the breeding season, when he is defending his territory, he takes on forestry Land-Rovers. He usually wins.

Emerging from the woods, the way follows the road for a short distance, crosses the bridge by the inviting Fiddichside Inn, and enters an attractive garden area which used to be the yard of Craigellachie railway station. There is another bridge here; a very beautiful one built by Thomas Telford in 1814. It is of cast iron, supported by castellated stone turrets, and, in spite of its elegant appearance, it was one of the few bridges to survive the ferocious spate of 1829, when the Spey rose by fifteen feet.

Telford Bridge, Craigellachie

TREE VERSUS DEER

FROM CRAIGELLACHIE the Speyside Way goes on to Ballindalloch, via Aberlour and Carron, but Molly Porter had suggested that we make our way to Dufftown taking a spur off the main route which follows the old Speyside railway line. The idea appealed to me and I accepted Molly's offer, but first I made a visit to Craigellachie Forest, where I had arranged to meet a lad called Tony Hinde.

Molly Porter

Tony had given me careful instructions as to our rendezvous, but I had a little difficulty in locating him, because he was fifteen feet up a tree. He is a forest ranger, and the device he was using is known as a high seat. It serves a dual purpose, in that it allows the observer to see over low-lying growth, and it raises him above the ultra-sensitive nose of the roe. The roe deer's eyesight is not of the best, but it has an incredibly keen sense of smell.

Tony Hinde is fascinated by the roe, and very sympathetic to it, but he told me that as the forests increase, so do the deer, and problems arise. The roe likes plenty of cover and also needs open spaces for feeding and the rut – the Craigellachie Forest is ideal. Once the trees have reached a reasonable size, they are fairly safe from the roe deer's attentions, although even then, bark stripping can be a nuisance. When the trees are young, however, they can easily be damaged by the bucks rubbing their antlers against them. More serious still is the browsing of the young plantings: the tops and outer branches are frequently nibbled and stripped, as the deer make a meal of the tenderest parts of the new growth.

The most obvious method of limiting the damage is regulation of the number of animals, but a simpler and very effective device is the tree shelter. This is a fairly recent invention and consists simply of a column of corrugated plastic slipped over the seedling, and anchored in place. It effectively and cheaply protects the young plant not only from the roe deer, but also from rabbits, which at this stage can be equally damaging. There are other advantages too. The tender young seedlings are protected from the wind and from smothering weeds, and inside the plastic container there is a mild mini-climate which encourages growth. I'm sure that Tony Hinde would rather handle plastic tree protectors than a gun.

THE SPUR

THE PART of the Way known as The Spur starts in the Fiddich Park at Craigellachie, and follows the old Speyside railway line to Dufftown. The original permanent way has been made into a fine footpath, but not without a great deal of effort, as Molly Porter explained. The railway ballast of the old line made for agonising ankle-cracking walking, and Molly organised the council lorry to deliver loads of quarry dust, which was taken in by wheelbarrow and spread along the route. It is now well packed into the stones of the ballast and provides a firm and well-drained path. The walk to the first of the Dufftown distilleries is only about four miles, and it's delightful all the way. The path goes through lovely mixed woodland and shrubbery, and small birds are everywhere. There are bullfinches, goldfinches, yellowhammers and warblers, and somewhere in the woods we could hear the hammering of a woodpecker. The river Fiddich is never far away, and it appears and disappears in the trees, first on the left, then the right, as it goes under one of the bridges.

Herons fish here, and we saw one rise up silently like a great grey ghost, the deceptively ponderous beat of the broad wings taking it quickly out of sight round a bend in the river. The watter waggies, pied and grey wagtails, bobbed and fluttered at the water's edge, and several times I caught sight of one of my favourite birds, the dipper or water ouzel. The dipper is a dumpy, thrush-sized bird, like a giant wren in contour, but in dark brown livery, with a startlingly white breast. It's a hyperactive little bird, with a constant bobbing or dipping motion which gives it its name. It also dips under the water, and seems as happy beneath the surface as above it. The bird drops, or simply walks, into powerful torrents with casual confidence, and finds its food among the weeds and stones, its feet giving it a secure grip on the bottom. The dipper always feeds facing upstream, and with head down and tail up, the pressure of the current counteracts its natural buoyancy.

The river is also home to mergansers and mallard, and is one of the remaining refuges for otters, which have been in decline in most parts of Britain. The otter is a beautiful and fascinating animal, and deserving of our care and protection.

There are sparrowhawks and buzzards here too, and Molly spoke to an old railwayman who remembered the buzzards nesting very close to the line. The same nest site had been in use for many years, and he always gave a toot on the whistle to see the bird rising from the tree. Molly was told of an accident in which a train had left the line and plunged down the bank. She was determined to find the place, and after much searching and scrabbling around in the undergrowth of the steep slope, she identified the spot by the coal which had been spilled from the engine's tender. Some of that historic coal found its way into the fire at Molly's cottage.

While the railway was in use, all the growth was cleared back from the track to reduce the fire risk, but Molly pointed out the species which were re-establishing themselves along the path. There were sycamore, alder, ash, beech, willow, rowan and dog rose, the fruit of which provides an autumn treat for the birds, and an oak tree about fifteen or twenty years old. Molly was especially proud of a solitary juniper clinging to the rock face of the old railway cutting, and was even able to take me to some apple trees. There are five species of apple along the track, and the belief is that they have sprung from cores thrown out by railway passengers. We searched long and hard for banana or orange trees, but had to make do with some wych elm.

Not far along the track there is a little complex of old buildings surrounding a strange structure known as the Popine Mill. The mill has a very striking pagoda-like roof, and its great water wheel was driven by a flow diverted from the Fiddich. When I first saw this place, I had fantasies of its being restored, possibly as some kind of hostel and craft centre, but the buildings are now in a poor state of repair, and, I believe, are under a demolition order.

I parted company with Molly by the Old Convalmore distillery, on the edge of Dufftown. I knew that it was unlikely we'd meet again for some time, for she was off to take up a post as ranger on the Pennine Way. As a mountaineer, Molly will be happy in the high places, but I know she will look back with affection on her time on Speyside, where her knowledge and commitment have been so valuable.

DUFFTOWN: SCOTTISH ATMOSPHERE AND A GOOD BADDIE

DUFFTOWN MARKS the real beginning of the whisky country, and the place is full of names which most people only see on bottles. It isn't a very big place, but it has no less than seven distilleries, each bearing a famous name; and an organised walkabout has been set up for visitors, in which trained guides attempt to explain the mysteries of the whisky industry. There is mystery aplenty, as I discovered when I dropped in at the Mortlach distillery. Mortlach is one of the names known to serious malt whisky drinkers, and among the people responsible for its quality are George Thomson, the distillery manager, and John Robson, who looks after the brewing.

I was treated to an entertaining and interesting tour of the premises, and, instructive as it was, I was left with two or three questions. If the whiskies produced in Dufftown were all Glenlivets, and from the same area, what explained the distinctive differences in flavour? George said that the water and the shape of the stills accounted for that, but when I asked why the shape of a copper container should change the taste, he cheerfully admitted that he didn't know. No one knew; but when one of the six stills had to be replaced, it had to be with one of exactly the same shape and capacity. When John was explaining the maturation process in old sherry casks, where the whisky darkens and takes extra flavour from the wood, I enquired, with deliberate naivety, why they didn't simply add some sherry to the whisky. Answer: 'It's been tried, and it doesn't work.' 'Why?' 'No one knows!' Both John Robson and George Thomson, expert as they are, accept that in the whisky process, if something works, that's explanation enough.

They did explain the difference in the flavour of Speyside and west coast malts. This happens mainly during the malting process, when the damp, germinating barley is being dried in the kilns. On the west coast, a good deal more peat smoke (about three times more than on Speyside) is allowed to impregnate the barley. This accounts for the deep smoky taste which appeals to the drinker of malt whiskies from the west coast highlands and islands. I asked John if he believed, as some people do, that the older the whisky the better. He believed that was true, but only up to fifteen years or so, after which time it can begin to acquire a woody taste from the cask. 'So, after fifteen, forget it?' I said. John looked quite horrified. 'No, no. Dinnae forget it, man. Drink it quick.'

The most alarming thing I learned about whisky is that around two per cent of all the stock maturing in casks evaporates through the wood into the atmosphere. When one considers that the Mortlach distillery alone has 26,000 100-gallon and 55-gallon casks in store, and that there are hundreds of distilleries all over the country, it's a wonder that birds can fly. It may explain why visitors to Scotland enthuse about the wonderful air.

James Duff, fourth Earl of Fife, founded Dufftown in 1817. It was originally called Balvenie, and Balvenie Castle still stands, as it has done since the thirteenth century. For about two centuries, the castle was in the hands of the Stewarts, and Mary, Queen of Scots is said to have spent a couple of nights here in 1562. Why not, indeed? She appears to have visited everywhere else. The Marquis of Montrose was here in 1644, and the Jacobite troops used the place after the battle of Killiecrankie in 1689. Nowadays, the tourists skim over these momentous events in their tours of the castle.

Dufftown also has connections with a well-known Scottish folk song. The clock tower at the centre of the town was built in 1839, and the famous clock is known as the clock that hanged MacPherson. James MacPherson was a seventeenth-century tearaway, highly thought of by the ordinary folk for his habit of succouring the poor and severely irritating the rich – the social and economic divisions of the time being even greater than they are today. He was known as the Scottish Robin Hood, but I prefer to think of Robin Hood as the English James MacPherson.

MacPherson was eventually apprehended and sentenced to death in Banff in 1700. Local inhabitants, mainly from the adjoining town of Macduff and from Banff itself, protested vigorously and a pardon was granted. The reprieve was on its way, when the sheriff of Banff, Lord Braco, who was not a special fan of MacPherson's, had the town clock advanced by an hour (the song says a quarter of an hour) and that was the end of a jolly career. It's said that MacPherson died in the same defiant manner in which he had lived. Below the gallows tree, he played a final tune on his beloved fiddle before smashing it to pieces. Folk singer Hamish Imlach feels that it would have made a better song had he played the double bass, and smashed it over the hangman's head. The legend has it that the clock in Banff has been a quarter afore ever since, but the fact is that clock was moved to Dufftown, and was kept at proper time – except in emergencies, of course.

MacPherson's Fareweel

'Fareweel ye dungeons dark and strang,
Fareweel, fareweel tae thee.
MacPherson's time will no be lang,
On yonder gallows tree.'

CHORUS:
Sae rantin'ly, sae wantonly,
Sae dauntin'ly gaed he.
He played a tune and he danced aroon,
Ablow the gallows tree.

'It was by a wumman's treacherous hand
That I'm condemned tae dee;
Below a ledge by a windae she stood,
And a blanket she threw ower me.'

CHORUS.

'Twas the Laird o' Grant, that Heilan' sant,
Who first laid hauns an me.
He played the cause on Peter Broon
Tae let MacPherson dee.'

CHORUS.

'Untie these bands frae aff my hands,
And gie tae me my sword,
And there's no a man in broad Scotland,
But I'll brave him at his word.'

CHORUS.

'There's some come here tae see me hanged,
And some tae buy my fiddle,
But before that I dae pert wi' her,
I'll brak her through the middle.'

CHORUS.

He took the fiddle intae baith o' his hauns,
And he brak it ower a stane;
Saying, 'Nae ither haun sall play on thee,
When I am deid and gane.'

CHORUS.

'Oh little did my Mither think,
When first she cradled me,
That I would turn a rovin' lad,
And dee on the gallows tree.'

CHORUS.

The reprieve was comin' ower the Brig o' Banff,
Tae set MacPherson free,
But they set the clock a quarter afore,
And hanged him tae the tree.

ABERLOUR:
RECORDS, PRICES AND PRIZES

ABERLOUR WAS founded in 1812 by Charles Grant of Wester Elchies, and its proper name is Charlestown of Aberlour. It lies on the banks of the Spey, and even here, in an area which takes great pride in the condition and cleanliness of its towns and villages, Aberlour is outstanding, and has won an award as the best large village in Scotland. It has the generously wide streets and low buildings which are typical of Speyside, and extravagant displays of flowers decorate the green in front of the beautiful old church. The old railway station yard is now a public park, and the station building itself is a very tastefully painted tea room. Needless to say, there is an Aberlour distillery, and fishing is of great importance.

On my first visit to Aberlour, I met Jimmy Milne who is a ghillie on the Spey, and on my second, I spoke to Jimmy Christie who has

49

Aberlour

a rather special interest in the river. Jimmy Milne is a bluff, talkative, ruddy-faced character with thirty years' experience on the Spey. Most of his clients are visitors to Scotland, well heeled and willing to pay fat fees for the privilege of fishing one of the world's great salmon rivers. It's Jimmy's job to make sure they go away with the desire to return. He prepares the rods in the morning, and advises on the choice of flies. In the spring, large tube flies are effective, and in the summer smaller flies are used for the grilse, or young salmon. Some of the fishers are elderly, and wading can be quite dangerous, as the river bottom is constantly changing, and this is where Jimmy's experience is of great help. I raised the question again of the salmon taking lures when they are not feeding in fresh water. Jimmy Milne agreed that healthy fish have been opened up and examined, and found to contain no food whatsoever. However, Jimmy has a theory that they crush the juices from small fish and crustaceans and reject the rest. I'd never heard that notion before, but it does seem incredible that a hefty, healthy fish can exist for months with no food at all. Jimmy is one of many who is worried about the decline in salmon numbers, and told me that it is beginning to have an effect on the hotels along the river valley.

Like the whisky trade, salmon fishing has its mystique, and when I asked Jimmy about the bewildering selection of exotically named and elaborately designed flies available to the angler, he quoted an old friend. In the bar of the Aberlour Hotel, he asked Johnny Smith, an old ghillie from Carron, what was the best fly to use at a certain time of year. The answer was, 'The best fly at any given moment is the one you happen to be using.' I also quizzed Jimmy about the stories we hear about giant fish, and while he accepted the angler's well-known capacity to believe his own fibs, he does remember some whoppers — fish that is, not fibs. In the stretch of water immediately opposite the village, a man called Jimmy Mays took a fish of $48\frac{1}{2}$ pounds, and about four feet long. Even that fish is dwarfed by one taken in 1922 on the Tay by Miss G. W. Ballantine, which scaled 64 pounds. Well over half a hundredweight of salmon; a record which stands to this day.

To meet Jimmy Christie, I had to find one of the less attractive corners of Aberlour: the coal yard. He had some interesting things to say in contrast to Jimmy Milne's stories of the hefty prices paid by his clients. Well over a hundred years ago, the people of Aberlour were granted free fishing rights on this part of the Spey by the then Laird of Carron. This right was enjoyed by the villagers until 1951, when it became a legal requirement to hold a permit to kill game fish. Jimmy and his colleagues then had to legalise the position of the local people, while still offering the fishing at a modest, affordable price. The running expense of £3500 per annum is raised by letting to strictly controlled numbers of outsiders. This is regulated by the water bailiff, and by the person who issues the permits, but the local people are always given priority; so, although the system has changed, Jimmy Christie and his team have ensured that the wishes of the old Laird have been observed, in essence.

STATIONS AND STILLS:
A CASTLE AND A COW

FROM ABERLOUR, the Way continues along the old railway line, the thick growth of trees, bushes and flowers always threatening to overcome and smother the narrow path. Rosebay willowherb is everywhere, and although it's a dreadful nuisance in a garden, it's a handsome plant in a place like this, with its tall cones of lilac-coloured flowers. The flowering whins add their colour, and later in the summer, their pea-like seed pods dry in the sun, until they scatter their seeds in an explosion which can make quite a startling pop on a quiet day. A variety of moths and butterflies are attracted to the knapweed, honeysuckle, ragwort, vetches, balsam, ragged robin, and thistles of various types. The most imposing of these is a large, beefy specimen known as the Scotch thistle. It is actually the French thistle, as any botanist will tell you.

Walter Scott virtually invented romantic Scotland, and among those who enthusiastically endorsed the fantasy was King George IV. Scott organised the King's ceremonial visit to Edinburgh, where his majesty adorned his generous bulk with extravagant tartans, and carried a large thistle. It was the wrong one, but he was the King after all, and that's how the French thistle came to be accepted as the Scotch thistle.

It always pays to go quietly in the country, and it's possible to see a great deal if one remains alert. Kestrels and buzzards are obvious along the Way, as they hang on the wind, or wheel in the open sky, but the sparrowhawk is normally only glimpsed as a blur, as it rockets between the trees with superb judgement and control. One of the sparrowhawk's favourite and most effective tricks is to zip low along a hedge, then suddenly flip over with lightning speed, to surprise small birds feeding on the other side.

The places along the Way are marked by disused railway stations which share their names with the distilleries. The main function of the Speyside railway was to serve the whisky trade, and some of the distilleries had their own sidings and loading bays. The old station at Tamdhu has been tastefully converted into an attractive visitors' centre, where people are given a warm welcome, and introduced to the mysteries, and the taste, of Tamdhu whisky.

The station at Carron, its blue sign now weathered and faded almost to invisibility, used to serve the Imperial distillery. Their buildings are now used only for storage, and what was once a bustling industrious village is today a sleepy, charming backwater.

At Ballindalloch, there stands what looks like a fairy castle. Someone's fantasy, a film set, a museum, a national monument, but it's a family home. The oldest part of the superb building is a tower

Ballindalloch Castle

which, the experts say, dates from the early sixteenth century; the date 1546 is carved on a lintel in one of the rooms. The MacPherson Grant family have occupied the castle throughout its history, and it is now lived in by Clare, daughter of Sir Ewan and Lady MacPherson Grant, her husband Oliver Russell, and their family.

Like many of the really ancient grand Scottish houses, Ballindalloch Castle has undergone many changes. In 1850 a courtyard and wings were added, and the main entrance was moved and made more imposing. Windows were redesigned, and stone pediments added which still bear the initials and crests of family members. Less than thirty years later, Sir John's son George got the itch, and added nine rooms to what was already, by ordinary standards, a fairly roomy house. It was Sir George who virtually invented a cow, by establishing the now world-famous herd of Ballindalloch black Aberdeen Angus cattle, whose descendants still graze the policies.

Sir George's additions were demolished in 1965, restoring the building to its original coherent plan. Clare and Oliver Russell, who were kind enough to allow me to have a look at Ballindalloch, appeared to be in love with the place, and I, for one, hope that they will not be tempted to make any further alterations. Ballindalloch Castle is just about perfect as it is.

BALLINDALLOCH:
CANOES AND A BONNIE FECHTER*

BALLINDALLOCH IS approached by the most substantial and impressive bridge I used along the route. This is the great viaduct which, although it dates back only to 1863, was so innovative in its design and building techniques that it has been scheduled as an ancient monument. I arrived at the old station of Ballindalloch on a perfect day. I had been feeling fine for the last few miles; the weather was ideal for walking, sunny with a bit of breeze, and I had been able to make good time. It was a pleasure to slow down here and take a look round.

There was plenty to enjoy. Through the girders of the viaduct, I watched a dipper walk from the rocks into the water, sometimes the feathers of the back still showing above the surface, sometimes submerging completely, to re-emerge some yards further upriver. The wagtail is an equally busy and active bird, but hunts above the river, fluttering and trotting along the stones, to make quick forays for the insects that haunt the bank. As I watched, dipper and wagtails moved further along the river, momentarily disturbed by four brightly coloured canoes. The canoeists were Clive Freshwater, his two young sons Gordon and Andrew, and his assistant Marjorie Ann Harper, known simply as M. A.

Clive Freshwater is known to several of my outdoor friends, and I had been keen to meet him for some time. He is a quietly spoken, athletically built fellow, who comes from Mablethorpe in Lincolnshire. Like many of the best of the incomers, Clive is more knowledgeable about, and certainly more interested in Scotland than most of the natives. He came to Glenmore Lodge in 1960 as an instructor in general outdoor skills, and after ten enjoyable years there, he left to set up his own water sports centre on Loch Insh, upriver from Ballindalloch. At first this centre catered for visitors in the hotels, in bed and breakfast accommodation, and in caravans, but then Clive and his wife Sally acquired the old church hall in Kincraig, and converted it into proper accommodation for 56 people. When it came to building his boat house on Loch Insh, Clive remembered

---

* *bonnie fechter* = brave fighter

'M.A.' and pupil

seeing logs used to good effect by the Cairngorm ski lift company. Logs of the size required were not easy to come by, and were expensive, so the boat house is built of redundant telegraph poles, bought by Clive near Dalwhinnie for £3.50 each and transported to Loch Insh.

From the beginning of his enterprise, Clive Freshwater found himself enmeshed in bureaucracy, but at Loch Insh permission was eventually gained from the Forestry Commission and from Inverness County Council to go ahead with the water sports centre. At Ballindalloch, where he opened his second centre, his troubles really began. His idea was to start his tyro canoeists off on the still water of the loch, and as they gained basic skills, to develop them on the River Spey. Not a man to waste time hanging around, he simply went ahead, only to find himself facing solid and well-organised resistance from a group called the Spey Fishery Trust. This was an amalgamation of representatives of the big estates along the river, and they certainly didn't intend to have this Sasunnach* upstart messing about on their river. It was in 1972 that Clive first put his canoes in the river, on the genuine, if naive, assumption that he had

---

* *Sasunnach* = English, foreigner, southerner

a right to do so. He was immediately given to understand that the river was private, no canoeing or boating was allowed, and there were no public rights whatsoever. An interdict was taken against him for the use of the water, and another against landing; both banks at Knockando being owned by the estate. Clive lay low for about two years, in the meantime quietly conducting his own experiments to see whether there really was any disturbance to the fish.

The Spey Fishery Trust obviously thought that Clive was totally outgunned, but they had chosen the wrong man, for, despite a spectacular lack of resources, he decided to fight it out in court. The case was a complex one, and involved two weeks of proof. It was assumed that no one would speak against the landowners, but Clive raised no fewer than twenty witnesses, including experienced river fishermen and two professional ghillies. One of the most impressive of these witnesses was Major Waddington who ran the fishing at Blairfindy Lodge, charging very substantial fees. He was the author of two definitive works on salmon fishing, and had had bestowed on him the ultimate accolade – a fly named after him. With the Waddington fly in his corner, Clive was beginning to have a fighting chance, and when ghillies and fishermen were prepared to say that it was quite feasible that a canoe passing over a pool could actually raise fish which had been inactive all day, things were looking better.

In his summing up in the Court of Sessions, Judge Lord Maxwell did not accept that there was damaging disturbance to the fishing; and on the question of right to use the river, established precedent was quoted, the river having been used by the Rothiemurchus estate, and the Glenfeshie wood company to float logs, as was Loch Insh. Ironically, the upriver estates had fought a similar case, from the opposite viewpoint, against the Duke of Richmond and Gordon in 1782. The Duke had the crown right to fish the mouth of the Spey with the use of cruives. The cruive was a dry stane dyke* built across the river, with very narrow openings at which the salmon were caught. The upper proprietors complained that the cruives obstructed the movement of timber, and the Duke of Richmond and Gordon was told to remove them. Clive's case was founded on the same public right to navigate, and the court found in his favour.

---

* *dry stane dyke* = a stone dyke or wall made without mortar

The case went to appeal at the Court of Sessions, and was rejected. It then went before a panel of five judges led by Lord Hailsham in the House of Lords. It was rejected. Many people, young and old, now enjoy their canoeing on the Spey, under Clive's instruction, and the former station at Ballindalloch has been converted into an excellent bunkhouse, only a few yards from the river bank.

PARTING OF THE WAYS: THE ABERNETHY FOREST

A T BALLINDALLOCH, the Speyside Way also ran into trouble with landowners. The Countryside Commission for Scotland had successfully negotiated with the railways, who still owned the old line which was to be the footpath, only to be informed that the estate had sold the ground for use as a railway, and not for walking, and still had the right to prevent any other use. That stalemate still exists, and the path from Ballindalloch onwards is completely overgrown and impassable. The walker is faced with the alternatives of making for Nethybridge, and through the Abernethy Forest and the Pass of Ryvoan to Glenmore Lodge (the proposed terminus of the Way), or following another footpath to Tomintoul. On my first visit, I took the former route.

Nethybridge is just south of Grantown-on-Spey, and the nearby Abernethy Forest is a delight for the walker and the naturalist. This is one of several Scottish remnants of the old Caledonian pine forests, and although this type of wood is now rare in Britain, it is still quite common in parts of Europe. There is a great belt of evergreen across Scandinavia and into northern Russia, and Scotland is at the western and southern edge of this boreal forest. In my book on the West Highland Way, I mentioned Caledonian pines at Glen Falloch, Loch Tulla, and in Glen Cononish, but the Abernethy Forest is much more extensive, and really more interesting.

The older trees here were seedlings when Bonnie Prince Charlie was at Culloden, but there is good natural regeneration on this site, and there are specimens of all ages. The natural pattern of growth in this wood (unlike commercial plantations) means that the trees create their own space, and the sun is allowed through to the forest floor, creating more rich growth; it also means that there is a great variety of species. In the more sheltered, lower parts of the wood, the granny trees, some of which are over three hundred years old, are massive specimens, but further out on the hill where they are more exposed, trees of the same age are much smaller and obviously having to struggle for existence. It was in the Abernethy Forest that I met up with Gordon Miller, who is a botanist and ecologist, and a real forest fanatic. He is particularly impressed by the variety in the Abernethy Forest, and pointed out the richness of growth in alder, birch, rowan, heather, bracken, blaeberries, and a profusion of juniper. It is this variety that makes the Abernethy Forest such a haven for wild life, and as well as red and roe deer, there are the fox and the badger, and the delightful little red squirrel. The giant capercaillie, the horse of the woods, struts and threatens intruders, and it's easy to see goldcrest, siskin and crossbill. Gordon told me that the whole area is wonderful for plants, and one can find the little white orchid, creeping ladies' tresses (he didn't specify whether it's the ladies or the tresses which do the creeping), and the rare orchid known as St Olaf's Candlestick.

The Abernethy Forest with its great variety of trees, well spaced and with a healthy underlayer of growth, looks entirely natural, but Gordon Miller warned me not to be deceived. There is evidence of activity here in the seventeenth century, though at that time, the forest was probably being exploited rather than managed. The real activity began in the eighteenth century, with the establishment of an iron foundry at Nethybridge. Iron ore was brought from the Lecht, and the trees were used for charcoal. There was much felling, but replanting too. In earlier times, the forests were often destroyed for fear of wolves and bears, and in 1746 a great fire did enormous damage at Abernethy. However, fire was not always disastrous, as it cleared thick undergrowth and created ideal conditions for seedling trees.

As I moved out into more open country, I made my rendezvous with Dave Gowans, a warden with the Nature Conservancy Council. Dave told me that we were now in the Cairngorm National Nature Reserve, the largest in Britain, and pointed out the changes in terrain and wildlife. It was a blisteringly hot day, and I was in shorts and stripped to the waist, but over on the Cairngorms, the great snowfields were still intact, and indeed, they sometimes last through the year. Dave's patch is mountain and moorland, in a subarctic habitat. He describes it as eagle country, wild, huge, desolate, and very difficult of access. The occasional stray snowy owl has been seen here, and regular nesters are the beautiful little snow bunting, and the dotterel. The dotterel is a tiny plover and nests in even higher and more remote places than the golden plover. This strange little bird is one of the few which displays fine colour and markings in the female, and rather dull, nondescript plumage in the male. Odder still, it is the male which does all the brooding and hatching of the

Golden Eagle

59

chicks. In the rigorous conditions of the high tops, uncovered eggs chill quickly, and the dotterel sits very tightly indeed. It has even been known to climb on to a human hand when the eggs were held in the palm. The Nature Reserve is a dramatic and spectacular place, and it's fitting that it should be the home of creatures like the great golden eagle, the peregrine falcon, and the Scottish wild cat.

RYVOAN: THE FAIRY LOCHAN AND THE WELL OF THE POTS

THE PASS of Ryvoan, which leads on to Glenmore Lodge, was formed by the great Cairngorm glacier, and the debris left behind formed dams which in their turn created lochs. As there was no natural feed to these lochs, they gradually disappeared, leaving only boggy depressions behind. The one survivor is the Lochan Uaine. The name means the little green loch, and it is the greenest of greens. Molly Porter showed me the lochan on a brilliantly sunny day, with the colour at its brightest, and although we know that the green comes from the heavy growth of algae, it is easy to understand the legend of the fairies staining the water by washing their clothes in it. Ryvoan is known as the pass of the thieves, from the days when the Lochaber reivers came from the Fort William area to explore the rich pickings of the Spey valley. This was their escape route, but eventually the local people grew tired of their shenanigans, and lay in wait for them in deep pits, from which the reivers were showered with arrows. Some of those pits still exist.

There are other pits too, but these are the wells used by the women and young people who brought the livestock up here to the shielings* for the summer grazing. Their utensils and cooking pots were too heavy to be carried back and forth, so they were buried by one of the wells, and unearthed each summer. That well is still known as *Fauran nam polt*, the well of the pots. The old Ryvoan farm cottage was restored by the Mountain Bothy Association, and is open to

---

* *shieling* = a rough or temporary hut or shelter

anyone who wishes to use it. The man who used to live there was a gem hunter and lapidarist, who once sold a particularly large smoky quartz stone to Queen Victoria. The Pass of Ryvoan is a truly beautiful place, and it is almost a pity to leave it for Glenmore Lodge and the end of this part of the walk.

A DALNASHAUGH CEILIDH*
AND UISGE BEATHA* AT GLENFARCLAS

I N T H E course of my walk I had established a loosely observed routine. I tried to make reasonable time, but was always prepared to stand and stare, or to invest time talking to and learning from interesting people along the Way. In the evenings, where possible, I had a hot bath, a meal, perhaps the occasional indulgence of a glass of the local malt, and went reasonably early to bed. The Dalnashaugh Hotel shattered all of that. It is Clive Freshwater's local watering

Dalnashaugh Hotel

* *ceilidh* = a social get-together, party   *uisge beatha* = whisky (the water of life)

hole, and I accepted his invitation to spend a quiet evening with some of the local folk. The proceedings were overseen by the enormously affable landlord Jimmy Thom, and his even more good-natured, and endlessly patient wife Nessa. The quiet evening turned out to be as relaxing as going ten rounds with Frank Bruno but, it must be said, much more fun. Clive produced his guitar and I produced mine, but I readily confess that we were soon outgunned by the local talent, which included traditional singer Willie Clark of Ballindalloch. I was familiar with Willie through folk festivals, and had featured his recordings on my radio programme, *Macgregor's Gathering*, but this was my first meeting with him, and I found a robustly built man who, though in his seventies, has a voice that could strip paint at fifty yards. He has an extensive repertoire of traditional songs, and the extrovert, show-off personality of the born entertainer. Great crack! George Anderson and Ian Duncan on accordion and bass supplied music for singing and dancing, and there were no end of people to keep things going. And keep them going

The author with Jimmy Thom and Tony the pony at Glenfarclas

they did, long after I had given up, knowing I had a busy day ahead.

I had arranged to visit the nearby Glenfarclas distillery the next day, and my admiration for Jimmy Thom increased immeasurably when I found him waiting for me in the morning in a beautiful trap drawn by an even more beautiful pony called Tony. This was Jimmy Thom's cure for a hangover – his, not mine – and before I had covered the few miles to the Glenfarclas distillery, I was wide awake and ready to face anything. What I did face was an absorbing tour of the place of origin of one of the world's great whiskies.

I was greeted at Glenfarclas by George Grant, the present chairman of the company, who with his son John as managing director, now oversees the manufacture of a product known all over the world. As Jimmy Thom and Tony the pony headed back for the Dalnashaugh, I asked George Grant about the old pagoda-shaped roof which was lying in the yard. It was obviously the traditional cover of a malt kiln chimney, and George explained that it was kept for purely sentimental reasons. Glenfarclas is a very modern complex, and gave up the malting process some time ago, the barley now being bought in. The Grants run one of a mere handful of family distilleries, and many of the people who work there had fathers and grandfathers at Glenfarclas.

> Of all the whiskies, malt is king.
> Of all the kings, Glenfarclas reigns supreme.

Those words were written by a rival distiller in 1912, but Glenfarclas goes much further back than that. Before the licensing and legalising of whisky production, distilling was a sideline of farming, and was looked on as a good way of using surplus barley, the resulting drink being used for home consumption. In 1836, a year before the crowning of Queen Victoria, John Grant, a local cattle breeder, bought a farm called Rechlerich, at Ballindalloch. Part of the package was the farm distillery, for which Grant had to pay £511. 19s. 0d. The Grants at that time were interested only in farming, and the distillery was sublet to a man called Smith, who later built the Cragganmore distillery. However, in the 1890s, John Grant's widow and his two sons John and George created the Glenfarclas Glenlivet Distillery Company, which, after many vicissitudes, reached the pre-eminence which it now enjoys. The last few years have been the best

Glenfarclas distillery

ever for Glenfarclas, with the market expanding in Britain, North America and Europe, and progress being made in Australia, New Zealand and the Far East. Not bad for a firm which cost £511. 19s. od.

The accoutrements of a distillery, even a modern one like Glenfarclas, are attractive, with gleaming brass and copper everywhere, and the huge exotic shapes of the stills looming overhead; so my tour, conducted by the boss, George Grant, was aesthetically satisfying. I was, however, sometimes bewildered by the flood of information showered on me by George, who knows the whole process backwards, forwards and sideways. One thing did become clear to me, and that was that despite the sophistication of the modern plant, the basics of whisky making remained as they were when George's ancestor first acquired Rechlerich farm more than a hundred and fifty years ago.

How to make whisky

First, borrow £511. 19s. od. to buy a distillery. You'll then require a supply of barley, peat and good – very good – water. The starch in the barley must be converted to sugar so that it will ferment, and this is achieved by a process called malting. The barley is steeped and softened in water for a few days, and then spread out and allowed to begin germination. The change from starch to sugar now takes place, with the grain being regularly turned over in a carefully controlled temperature. As the grain begins to sprout, the maltster uses very fine judgement to decide when the germination should be halted. This is done by spreading the material on a wire mesh, and drying it over a peat fire. The peat smoke absorbed by the drying grain plays a crucial part in the flavour of the finished product. On Speyside, the smoke is carefully controlled, whereas in the highlands and islands of the west, the whiskies are produced with a much peatier flavour. Like most of the bigger modern distilleries, Glenfarclas now buys its barley already malted, but to a very specific standard.

The barley, each grain now with a little shoot, and dried and subtly flavoured by the peat smoke, is ground into flour, known in the trade as grist. It is then mixed with hot water in a vessel called a mash tun, the resulting porridgy mess being described as mash. After a time the sweet liquid (wort) is drained away, and the remains of the grist are disposed of. At one time, this residue was a clue to the existence of an illicit still, as it was usually dumped in the nearest burn, staining the water. It also had, and has, a rather pungent smell. Nowadays this waste, which is known as draff, is processed for animal feed.

From the mash tun, we now have a rich, sugary liquid which is ready for the fermentation process. Yeast is added, and the liquid is now called wash, as the sugar is converted into alcohol. George Grant invited me to take a sniff of the air over the washbacks – the containers containing the fermenting liquid. I rashly took in a hefty lungful which left me coughing and spluttering, and my eyes streaming from the carbon dioxide gas given off during fermentation.

Now comes the step which changes the wash – the fermented liquid – into whisky. This is the distillation, and it takes place in the huge copper pot stills; not once, but twice. The first distillation produces liquid known as low wines, but when this is put through the still once again – the spirit receiver this time – we almost have whisky. I say *almost*, because although the spirit is very carefully selected, with the spirit at the beginning and end of the distillation being rejected, the liquid that is left is a perfectly clear, colourless and rather characterless product.

It has to grow up, and after water has been added to reduce the alcohol content, it is transferred to oak sherry casks, where, at the Glenfarclas distillery, it will remain for no less than eight years. There are also whiskies of twelve, fifteen, twenty-one and even twenty-five years old, and during the time that the whisky matures, it takes a deeper colour and richer flavour from the old oak sherry casks.

I hope that you have understood all this, for even with an expert like George Grant for my guide, it took me quite some time to grasp the principles. I had the pleasure of ending my instruction with a visit to the Glenfarclas visitors' centre, where Shirley Milne, the head guide, poured me a glass of very elderly Glenfarclas – 105° proof, and smooth as honey. So, I shall wish you a belated 'Slàinte Mhath'.

Donald Don

A song about a man with his own ideas on making whisky.

CHORUS:

Hirum ho for Donald Don,
Wi' a' his tanterwallops* on;
He's a lad that's worth the knowin',
For he maks heilan' whisky.

When first he cam' tae auld Dundee,
'Twas in a smoky hole lived he;
Whaur gauger* bodies couldnae see,
He made his heilan' whisky.

CHORUS.

When he was young and in his prime,
He lo'ed a bonny lassie fine;
She jilted him and aye sin syne*,
His only love is whisky.

CHORUS.

A bunch o' rags is a' his braws,
His heathery wig wad fricht the craws;
His dirty face and clorty* paws,
Wad foul the Bay o' Biscay.

CHORUS.

He has a sark*, he has but ane,
Fairly worn tae skin and bane;
Loupin'* like tae rin its lane,
Wi' fleas sae bauld and frisky.

CHORUS.

So here's a health tae Donald Don,
Wi' a' his tanterwallops on;
May he never lack a scone,
While he maks heilan' whisky.

CHORUS.

---

* *tanterwallops* = tattered clothes   *gauger* = exciseman
aye sin sine = ever since then   *clorty* = dirty   *sark* = shirt   *loupin'* = infested,
jumping, crawling

CHAPELTON OF GLENLIVET AND
A SECRET COLLEGE

WAY BACK at Spey Bay, and at many points along the way, the landmark which kept catching my eye was Ben Rhinnes, and I nursed a notion that I'd rather be looking down from it than looking up at it. At Glenfarclas I realised that I was very close to the hill, and set off for a closer look. Ben Rhinnes is lovely, with two peaks, one much lower than the other, and there is a rough but easily negotiable track which leads up the shoulder in a long, but not too heavy pull. On the lower part of the hill, the path is bordered by rank heather, blaeberries and lichens, and there are birch and rowan aplenty, as well as a sprinkling of conifers. A buzzard was mewing overhead, grouse were churring and shouting, 'Go back, go back,' and as I rounded a bend in the track, a startled stag and his hinds took off over the brow of the hill at an astonishing pace. The day was glorious, and the air diamond sharp, and as I began to make my way down from the summit, the whole of the Glenlivet area lay sharply etched below me like a highly coloured contour map.

I had a rendezvous at Chapelton of Glenlivet, but on the way, I called at Tombae farm. This is a beautiful place, and it's difficult to believe that it was tumbledown and derelict in 1979, when it was bought by Gordon Mackay. Gordon is a sheep farmer, and he and his wife took on this daunting project because they admired the situation, and welcomed the chance to restore a fine old farm and steadings. They hunted for slates, stones and lintels, and did most of the donkey-work on their own. The result is a superb farm which won an award from the Countryside Commission for Scotland. The winters here are long and hard; spring and the lambing come late; but the Mackays love the place, and when the days lengthen and the glen lights up, it is indeed idyllic.

A long moorland walk down from Ben Rhinnes brought me to the Braes of Glenlivet, and at Chapelton of Glenlivet, I met Sir Edward Peck. Sir Edward, a spare, fit man in his seventies, is retired from his service with NATO, and is now happy exploring and writing about Glenlivet, Avonside, and the surrounding country. I joined up with him at the old schoolhouse of Chapelton. It had an

Sir Edward Peck

active life of a hundred years, but has been lying unused since 1960. It's a simple but attractive building, and it seems a pity that no one can take on its restoration, as it would make a fine house. In much better condition, and immediately adjacent to the school, is the old catholic church, with a tall tower and a lovely studded and heavily hinged front door. The chapel has a fine painted ceiling, and there are two tablets in memory of the Abbé Paul McPherson, who in 1812 was sent to the fortress of Savona, to inform Pope Pius VII, who was imprisoned there by Napoleon, that the British were coming to release him.

This whole area was a stronghold of Catholicism during the Reformation, and there was great support from the Dukes of Gordon. Sir Edward told me about a secret centre of resistance near here, and we decided to walk out and see it. No more than a few hundred yards from the pretty little chapel stand the very modern buildings of the award-winning Chivas Regal distillery. The complex still looks a little raw and stark in this mellow old landscape, but it's obvious that a great deal of trouble has been taken with the design and layout. There is a deliberate echo of the design of the chapel, and there is even the traditional pagoda-style malt kiln roof. This is decorative rather than functional, as a modern distillery such as this will use pre-malted barley. About a mile further on, we left the tarmac at a place called Eskemulloch, and followed a rough, broken and rather muddy track for another mile or so. Then quite suddenly, in a little fold in the hills, we found the old buildings of Scalan.

Chivas Regal distillery

Scalan

Scalan derives from the Gaelic for a turf-covered hut or shelter, and here, in this remote spot, in 1717, was founded a seminary for the training of priests. Between the 1715 and the 1745 Jacobite rebellions, the college was repeatedly sacked by the Hanoverians, and it was burned by Cumberland after Culloden. Another building was raised nearby, and in the eighty years of Scalan's existence, around a hundred priests were trained here, to be sent to various parts of the world. It was sheer dogged determination that kept the place going and the faith alive. The first Scottish priests to emerge after the Reformation were trained here in this tiny and remote place, and in 1777 Bishop Geddes, who was rector of Scalan for eleven years, wrote. 'The time, by the goodness of God, will come when the Catholic religion will again flourish in Scotland, and then, when posterity shall enquire, with a laudable curiosity, by what means any sparks of the true faith were preserved in these dismal times of darkness and error, Scalan will be mentioned with veneration, and all that can be known about it be recorded with care.'

SHRINKING MOUNTAINS AND THE LECHT

SAYING GOODBYE to Sir Edward Peck, I started off up the hill which separates Scalan from the Lecht glen. As I plodded upwards, there was a noticeable change in the growth underfoot, and as I reached the summit, there was nothing more than a couple of inches high, even the heather creeping close to the ground. On the west coast, at this height – about 2000 feet – the growth would still be quite healthy, but here, in a subalpine climate, a short growing season, and continuous scouring winds, the plants have to keep their heads down if they are to survive. With the sun still bright and the wind stinging my ears, it was pleasant to stop for a blow, and look back at Ben Rhinnes, now almost at eye level, and away beyond that, the Spey valley and the whole extent of my walk. Below me, and hidden in a fold in the hills, was Scalan, and Tomintoul looked like a sharply modelled toy village in the strong light. The most striking part of this huge panorama lay over to the west, in the endless ranges and peaks of the Cairngorms. From this distance, great snowfields looked like little patches of white, and I could clearly pick out Ben Avon, with its towers of rock; my ultimate destination.

The Cairngorms have shrunk. Over millions of years, the jagged crags have been rounded and polished and worn down from their original near Himalayan bulk. Nevertheless, they still form the highest mountain massif in Britain, with no less than six summits over 4000 feet; the huge Beinn Macduibh (Ben Macdui), at 4296 feet standing second only to Ben Nevis's 4408 feet. The climate here is an Alpine one, and apart from the lower, more sheltered glens and corries, the terrain supports a specialised group of plants and wild creatures. The Cairngorms are beloved of the Alpine plant enthusiast, and the red grouse of the heather moors is replaced on the high tops by the ptarmigan, while the brown hare gives way to the blue, or mountain hare. Both the ptarmigan and the mountain hare turn white in the winter, the camouflage protecting them from their predators the eagle, the fox, and the peregrine falcon. On the lower slopes, that dashing little falcon, the merlin, preys on the pipits and ring ouzels.

The winter climate here is very severe indeed. The terrain is only for the most hardy and experienced, and many more folk come to grief through exposure than from falls. People will still go into the mountains, nevertheless; for the sheer grandeur and beauty of a place like this is irresistible.

An easy descent from my windy vantage point brought me down into the Lecht, with its winding stream and masses of juniper bushes,

The Lecht iron mine

and I for a while stopped to take a few photographs of the old iron mine building. Mining in the Lecht goes back to 1730, when ore was transported to Coulnakyle, near Nethybridge, where it was smelted using wood from the Abernethy Forest. All the ore was carried on horseback.

The mine was abandoned in 1737, and lay in disuse until it was reopened by the Duke of Richmond about a hundred years later. The Duke was more interested in the rich seams of manganese, and these proved to be economically more viable. A crushing mill was built, and the stream was dammed and diverted to provide power, while two pairs of huge mill wheels, over 25 feet in diameter, were brought from Aberdeen and hauled up over the Lecht by horses. Horses were again used to take the crushed ore to Portgordon, 45 miles away, and from there by ship to Newcastle. The mine finally closed in 1846, in the face of competition from manganese imported from Russia.

THE WELL OF THE LECHT AND THE MONOCLED MUTINEER

THE SUMMIT of the Lecht, at just over 2000 feet, is now the site of the Lecht Ski Company. There is a large car park, a restaurant, ski tows, and all the accoutrements of such a place. Needless to say there was considerable resistance to the complex, but

Lecht ski centre

Jim McIntosh, who manages the place, has persisted, and while proving that the damage to the alpine plant life of the area is not as serious as was thought, provides a recreational facility for a great many people. As I left the Lecht glen at the lower end, I joined the road to Tomintoul, and came upon a road sign dating from 1754. Writing about the West Highland Way, I mentioned the road building of the English redcoats under General Wade and Major Caulfield, and it was interesting to come upon evidence of their activities here on the other side of the country. There is a little well by the roadside, and set into the rocks behind it is a flat stone carved with the words:

> *A ... D 1754*
> Five Companes
> Te 33rd. Regment
> Right Honle Lord
> Chas Hay. Colonel
> Made te road from
> here to te
> *SPEY*

They weren't so hot at spelling but they certainly knew their road building, for the road to Tomintoul follows almost exactly the route originally chosen by their surveyors.

74

Well of the Lecht

Only a few hundred yards from the sign, there is a very ordinary little cottage below the road, on the right and across a little burn. This modest and now deserted place became nationally famous in 1920, when it was the scene of a Wild West type shoot out. The gunman was Percy Toplis, who featured as the Monocled Mutineer in the BBC television series of that name. Toplis was involved in an army mutiny at Étaples and sentenced to death, but escaped and lived as a fugitive for some time. He was a skilled con man, and expert in the use of disguise; so much so, that he was able to re-enlist in the army, and served with considerable courage as a stretcher bearer before finally deserting.

In 1920, he murdered a taxi driver in Hampshire and went on the run once again. How he arrived in a remote cottage in the Lecht, no one knows. The television series used a certain degree of artistic licence, and the newspapers didn't get it quite right, but there is an official report by one George Greig, a policeman of the Banffshire constabulary, who served four years in Tomintoul.

Greig states that in response to a complaint from John McKenzie, a gamekeeper employed by the Duke of Richmond and Gordon, about a man who had been staying in the cottage and burning fence posts, he went to the Lecht, accompanied by McKenzie and John Grant, a farmer of Badnafrave. In the years after the war, there were

75

The Toplis cottage

vagrants wandering around all over the country, and neither the police officer nor his two companions had any reason to suspect that they were dealing with anything more serious.

They found Toplis half dressed and asleep. They woke him, intending to challenge him with trespass and the burning of some chairs. Toplis sprang to the wrong conclusion, went into an adjoining room, and returned brandishing a firearm. Greig, whose subsequent behaviour suggests that he was a tough customer and a brave man, was hit by a 45 calibre bullet which grazed the top of his collarbone, hit the shoulder blade, and was deflected downwards into his body. Grant sustained a stomach wound, while McKenzie miraculously escaped unscathed.

Toplis then made off over the Lecht by bicycle, a considerable feat in itself. The bicycle had been stolen in Ross-shire, and a bill still exists for a repair which was done in Tomintoul by the local blacksmith who thought Toplis was such a pathetic-looking specimen that he gave him half a crown. His repair bill was never paid. The gunman made his way to Aberdeen and headed south, but at Penrith, he was apprehended by the police and shot dead. His mother, when called to identify the body, said, 'He was just bad all his life.'

TOMINTOUL: THE HILL OF THE BARN AND THE WANGYE CAT

MY ARRIVAL in Tomintoul coincided with the annual highland games, which was a tremendous stroke of luck, for although Tomintoul's games may not be the biggest in Scotland, they are most certainly among the best. The situation is quite superb, the games field being bordered by old trees with occasional gaps providing windows out on to the fine scenery which surrounds the village. The games were established in 1824, and such is their reputation that athletes, dancers and musicians of international reputation are attracted quite regularly, despite the relative remoteness of the venue.

I am an unrepentant addict of the highland games. I love the good humour, the noise and bustle, the colour and sheer uninhibited fun. Fiercely competitive pipers play strathspeys, jigs and reels, and more seriously the piobaireachd*. The first category of music is known as the ceòl beag – literally, the little music. The second, the ceòl mór, or big music, is the classical music of the great highland bagpipe, as complex and subtle as an Indian raga. There are tiny girls, little more than toddlers, attempting with furious concentration to look as elegant as their big sisters, in the intricate steps of the Scottish dances. Kilted giants throw trees and huge chunks of metal around. The local bigwigs pose in their tartan finery. The occasional tearful child gets temporarily lost, dogs bark, the tea tent does a roaring trade, the whisky tent does even better, and everyone has a terrific time.

Almost everybody has heard of Tomintoul because of that endlessly repeated warning on the weather report, 'The A939 from Cock Bridge to Tomintoul is closed at the Lecht because of snow.' In fact, by the time that warning goes out, the lads at the ski centre have had it cleared, on most occasions. Another widely held misconception about the village is that it is the highest in Scotland. Tomintoul is pretty high, at 1150 feet above sea level, but it is beaten by the lowland village of Wanlockhead at 1350 feet.

The name of the village derives from the Gaelic, *Tom an t'sobhail*, the hill of the barn, or Barnhill. By the middle 1800s, the Gaelic

---

* *piobaireachd* = the classical music of the bagpipes

In Tomintoul – pipers

language was already in decline in the area, and now exists only in the place names. Queen Victoria was a bit scathing about Tomintoul in 1860, describing it as poor-looking and tumbledown. I think she'd be a bit more amused by it now, for the buildings are low and well made of attractive stone; the streets are wide and spacious, and laid out in the grid pattern of the planned village, thanks to the fourth Duke of Gordon. There is a lovely village square with benches and trees, and a water fountain which carries the invitation, 'Bairns, step up'. The fountain was presented to the village by an old 'Towler' called Robert Grant, as a memento of his boyhood in the village.

Tomintoul has a particularly fine tourist office and museum; the former presided over by the charming and hospitable Mima Foster and Margaret Irvine. Georgie McAllister is the museum assistant, and she combines a warm and attractive personality with a genuine knowledge of, and interest in the museum and the surrounding area. Most of the exhibits have been contributed by local people, and there is a splendid display of domestic and agricultural items, as well as a complete blacksmith's shop.

Probably the most intriguing exhibit in the museum is a stuffed and mounted specimen of the legendary, and some think, mythical, Moray black cat. The animal is big, more than three feet from head to tail, jet black but with whitish guard hairs, long legged, and it is said, more powerful than a normal wild cat or a domestic specimen. There is much current interest in the animal, and scientists are speculating about a hitherto unknown species, but older folk in the area say that the cats have been around for generations. Seventy-eight-year-old Jock Douglas of Forres can't understand what all the fuss is about, as he remembers his grandfather saying that the animal, which he knew as the Wangye cat, was well known around the village of Dallas. (Yes. This is the original Dallas.) Some people maintain that the Wangye is a rather large feral farm cat which just happens to be black; the scientists are interested but cautious; and the older folk just know that it's a quite different animal, and that it's been in the area for a long time. Jock Douglas says, 'They're big bonny looking animals and Dallas has known them as neighbours for generations. The Wangye is like an old friend.'

DELNABO AND STRAY MACGREGORS: ESTATES AND RESERVES

I WAS NOW approaching the end of my journey, which I had decided was to be on the summit of Ben Avon, but before tackling that, I had a prearranged meeting in Glen Avon with a man called Adam Watson. The way from Tomintoul took me by the beautiful Delnabo House on the Ailnack Water. Delnabo marks the site of an ancient meal mill. Clan Macgregor, which is usually associated with Argyll and Perthshire, have a long history in the area; they were known here as far back as the fifteenth century. In the seventeenth, the Earl of Moray brought Macgregors in to help put down clan Chattan, who had been giving him trouble. Later, some of the Macgregors who had been dispossessed of Glenlyon and Glenstrae by clan Campbell, and others who had problems with the Colquhouns, found their way here. In 1631, a chief of the clan, Gregor Macgregor, married the widow of one of the locally power-ful Grants, and thereafter, the names of Gordon, Grant and Mac-gregor were virtually interchangeable. Descended from these Strathavon Macgregors were a chief justice of Jamaica, and a governor of Newfoundland.

The walk from Delnabo to the foot of Glen Avon is a short but most enjoyable one, and not far along there is a sign which indicates the beginning of the Glen Avon estate. It extends for over twenty miles to Ben Macdui, and at one time was even bigger. The Cairngorms have Britain's biggest national nature reserve. It is managed by the Nature Conservancy Council, and the Royal Society for the Protection of Birds has acquired the upper part of the Glen Avon estate, an area of 5300 acres. The great plateau between Cairn Gorm, 4084 feet, and Ben Macdui at 4296, is the greatest expanse of high ground in Britain. The climate is very severe, with a consequent scarcity of life, and there was some protest at tax-payers' money providing a profit to a private estate for ground which was really of very little use to that estate. The counter argument was that although this type of habitat could provide nothing like the density and variety of plant, animal and bird life to be found in a good wood or estuary, for example, it was the very special nature of the region which made it valuable.

Ptarmigan, dotterel and golden plover all nest here, and all are preyed on by the golden eagle and peregrine, though the eagle probably depends mainly on the mountain hare for his sustenance. In spite of its wildness, its noble appearance and magnificent powers of flight, the eagle is quite happy to feed on carrion. This is one of the features which made the bird so vulnerable to trapping and

The author with Adam Watson

poisoning, before it was protected by law. The plant life is, of necessity, of the ground-hugging variety, and creeping azaleas and moss campion can be seen, as well as several Alpine rarities.

Ownership of this ground by the Royal Society for the Protection of Birds means that it can be protected in perpetuity, and it has already been seen that national nature reserves on private estates are very vulnerable. On Cairn Gorm, the extension of skiing into Lurcher's Gully, which adjoins the National Nature Reserve, was refused. In Glenshee, on the other hand, a ski tow was built, despite strenuous opposition by the Nature Conservancy Council. And so the struggle goes on for constructive compromise, if not outright co-operation, between the sporting estates, the farmers, the climbers and hill walkers, the tourists, and the naturalists and conservationists.

WITH A TERRESTRIAL ECOLOGIST IN GLEN AVON

A MAN WHO understands and helps to resolve environmental problems is Adam Watson, who works with the Institute of Terrestrial Ecology. Adam was to accompany me on the seven-mile walk from the beginning of the glen to the shooting lodge at Inchrory, and I could not have had a better companion. Adam's knowledge of countryside matters is endless, and his interest in wildlife profound. I keep my eyes and ears wide open outdoors, but Adam noticed, and could explain things which would undoubtedly have escaped me. As I crossed the wooden footbridge over the River Avon, I had observed five salmon idling at the bottom of a pool. The water was about fifteen feet deep, yet the fish and every detail of the stones on the river bed were clearly visible. Adam explained that the Avon runs over limestone and granite, and that, even in spate, there was very little of the peat which gives so many Scottish rivers their tawny brown colour. There is an old rhyme which says,

> *The Waters o' Avon they rin sae clear,*
> *Twad beguile a man o' a hundred year.*

Glen Avon is well loved by outdoor people, and has been described as the most perfect glen in Scotland. It's certainly one of Adam Watson's favourite places, and I could see why, for every time we turned a bend, there was a change of prospect. The limestone which accounts for the clarity of the river also gives the glen an unusual richness and fertility. This was demonstrated by the rich growth of birch, alder and rowan in the lower parts of the estate. Rabbits and hares were plentiful, and there were small birds everywhere. I was delighted that there were so many redpolls, one of my favourites among the finches; and a little farther up the glen, where we stopped for coffee and a bite, there was the biggest concentration of juniper I have seen in Scotland. 'Almost Scandinavian,' said Adam. The juniper berry is used to make gin, and in Scandinavia, a fine liqueur is produced from the cloudberry, which is also common here.

As we moved on, the character of the glen gradually changed. The birch and alder were left behind, and heather began to take over from the lush green. We came upon the remains of some old shielings, the shelters used by the people who brought their cattle up here for the summer grazing, and Adam had already pointed out a number of deserted farm houses and steadings along the glen. The people who lived here were not the victims of clearance, as elsewhere, but simply moved away in search of a better and easier way of life.

Just before I parted company with Adam, we had a rare treat. We were watching a small group of deer making their way over the brow of a hill, when a great dark bird sailed across. An eagle. It was identifiable as an immature bird by the blotchy plumage, and we watched as it sailed away in a leisurely fashion towards Ben Avon. I was to see the same bird several times before I left, but the thrill of that first sighting, with the red deer on the hill in the background, was something special.

A MAN OF THE HILLS AND A HIGH POINT

THE NEXT best thing to making a journey like this alone, is to make it with someone like Adam Watson, whose insight and knowledge, as well as his empathy with the countryside, make the whole experience so much more interesting and enjoyable. I was heading for the lodge at Inchrory, and I left Adam near the Linn of Avon, where the water drops about fifteen feet to run through a narrow rocky gorge. In the season, this is where the salmon can be seen, making their spectacular leaps from the holding pool, as they fight their way up to the spawning grounds.

The sharp change in direction of the River Avon at Inchrory was caused by glacial action, and the fine lodge house stands in a commanding position at the turn of the river. Inchrory was once a crossroads and meeting place for the old cattle reivers, and later for the drovers. It is now the centre of the sporting estate of Glen Avon, and it was here that I met John McDonald, the head keeper and estate manager. John is a vastly experienced outdoor man, who proved to be very helpful and informative, and, like Adam Watson, a useful companion on the hill. He told me that the estate now encompasses 42,000 acres, and at the last count by the Red Deer Commission, supported around 1800 animals: a good figure, and again, a result of the vein of limestone which gives the area its fertility.

The fences around Inchrory carried the antlers of a hundred stags; one season's kill. My attention was drawn to a fourteen-pointer, known as an imperial, but when I suggested that John must be pleased with that one, he soon put me right. The really good heads are left on the hill to breed, and it is the old, the infirm, diseased or deformed animals which are taken. Overstocking on this kind of terrain, and in this climate, results in animals dying in the winter, so that culling of both stags and hinds is necessary. On the Glen Avon estate, the animals are given a supplementary winter diet of hay and cattle cake, on the lower, more sheltered ground.

I learned quite a lot about antlers from John McDonald, including the fact that my imperial was a mess. 'What I'd call an ugly, inferior, goat-like head, Jimmie.' I thought he meant me for a minute, but he pointed to the excessive height and narrowness of the antlers, and the irregularity of the points. Perfect balance, and a broad spread are what is sought. The points, from the head up, are known as the brow, bay, trey, and tops, and John could tell an amazing amount about an animal's age and condition from the growth of antler. In a young vigorous beast, the brow points rise up in a strong curve, and in the older animal, they will point straight forward, or droop over the eyes. Another clue is that as the stag ages, the points of the tops diminish and become irregular, and disappear year by year. The thing which astounds me more than any other, is that these huge growths, representing a tremendous output of energy and material, are shed and regrown every year.

John McDonald's workplace on the Glen Avon estate is one of the highest in Scotland, much of the ground being over 3000 feet. It was with some trepidation, therefore, that I set out with him for the summit of Ben Avon at 3843 feet. John is well over six feet tall, built like a bedspring in a snakeskin, and though well into his fifties, is lean and fit. Sheer Glasgow cussedness kept me close behind him as we started the long slog upwards over the rough ground, and I was determined not to let his heels out of my sight. I suspect that he adjusted his pace to suit, and I knew also that he could keep going like this over a long day. In the stalking season he does just that.

On the lower slopes, we passed a line of grouse butts, and I learned that of the three main interests of the estate, grouse, salmon and deer, the grouse demanded the greatest output of time and hard work. Access tracks, as well as the butts, have to be maintained; the birds require a certain amount of cosseting and protection; and there is the regular autumn heather burning. This is to encourage the growth of new young green shoots for food, although areas of tall rank heather

John McDonald

Trophies at Inchrory

have also to be maintained for shelter and nesting. The main predator of the nesting grouse is the fox, and John told me he was quite happy about the eagles in the glen and on the hill. Their prey is mainly the hare – much easier to take than a grouse, which flies like a rocket from one patch of impenetrable, tangled heather to another.

Ben Avon, though much bigger than Ben Rhinnes, resembles that mountain in that it consists of a long, broad, rising ridge, punctuated by outcrops and towers of rock. The first of these on Ben Avon is Clach Bhan, known to John as the fairy rocks. On the top of the tor, there are bowl-shaped depressions, the fairy rings, which have been ground out by ice and weather, and it's said that pregnant women used to bathe in the icy water contained in these depressions. The belief was that this would guarantee an easy birth.

Red Deer

Loch Avon

I should have thought that an instant one would have been more likely, if the climb up the mountain hadn't already achieved that result. Before we reached Clach Bhan, we were already walking in a few inches of snow, though the air was vibrant, the sky flawlessly blue, and the visibility such that over the shoulder of the hill, the great bulk of Beinn a Bhuird – the table mountain – was clearly visible.

The summit was to be the climax of my long walk, and my heart sank as I realised that we were about to experience one of those sudden changes of weather for which this area is known and, in winter, feared. John felt that we should get off the hill as soon as possible, but as we talked, everything cleared as quickly as it had blackened. The stinging flurry of snow passed on in a rush, the lowering darkness gave way to brilliant sunshine and bright blue, and the high point of Ben Avon became the high point of my whole walk.

Looking across the Spey valley towards the Cairngorms

I looked back along the miles; down Glen Avon to Ben Rhinnes, and beyond that the richness of the Spey valley, and the distant villages of the Moray coast where I had begun. I felt grateful for the opportunity, and the health and strength, to have enjoyed this beautiful part of this most beautiful country.